THE COUNTRY SHEPHERDS

D0937457

Harold L. Longenecker

GROWING LEADERS BY DESIGN

How to Use Biblical Principles for Leadership Development

kregel
RESOURCES

Grand Rapids, MI 49501

To John S. Hiestand,
a leader to emulate, a mentor to honor,
a colleague to cherish, and a friend forever.

I express my thanks to Milo
Nussbaum and Doug Habegger for
so kindly assisting with chapter 8.

And to Esther, my wife,
more "thanks" than I can count.

Growing Leaders by Design: How to Use Biblical Principles for Leadership Development by Harold L. Longenecker.

Copyright © 1995 by Oak Hills Fellowship.

Published by Kregel Resources, an imprint of Kregel Publications, P. O. Box 2607, Grand Rapids, MI 49501. Kregel Resources provides timely and relevant resources for Christian life and service. Your comments and suggestions are valued.

Cover and Book Design: Alan G. Hartman

Library of Congress Cataloging-in-Publication Data
Longenecker, Harold L.
   Growing leaders by design: how to use biblical principles for leadership development / Harold L. Longenecker.
        p.   cm. (The country shepherds workshop series)
     Includes bibliographical references.
      1. Christian leadership—Study and teaching.
2. Rural churches. 3. Small churches. I. Title.
II. Series: The country shepherds workshop series.
BV652.1.L66   1995   253—dc20   95-8345
                                                                                CIP
ISBN 0-8254-3131-X (paperback)

1 2 3 4 5 Printing / Year 99 98 97 96 95

Printed in the United States of America

Contents

Foreword 5
Introduction 7

Section One—Patterns in Conflict

Chapter 1:   The Pattern of Society 15
Chapter 2:   The Pattern of Jesus 27

Section Two—The Pattern of Jesus
Applied to the Disciples

Chapter 3:   Leading Them to Believe 41
Chapter 4:   Helping Them to Grow 49
Chapter 5:   Teaching Them to Relate 57
Chapter 6:   Stimulating Them to Aspire 65

Section Three—The Pattern Confirmed

Chapter 7:   The First-Century Witness 73
Chapter 8:   The Contemporary Witness 83

Section Four —The Pattern at Work

Chapter 9:   Leading As We Grow .93
Chapter 10:   Leading As We Relate 105
Chapter 11:   Leading As We Aspire 117
Chapter 12:   Leading As We Influence 127
Chapter 13:   The Payoff 139

Appendixes

Appendix 1:   Designing a Pastoral Mentoring Ministry . . .151
Appendix 2:   Pastoral Mentoring and
              Leadership Transitions 158

Foreword

One of the things rural and smaller churches do best is grow leaders. A church I served grew to one hundred in its first fifty years and produced nine foreign missionaries, seven pastors, and three Christian college professors. Laymen who went out from that church into larger, urban churches often reported back to us that most of the leaders in those churches had their ministry starts in small, rural churches. Churches have unique opportunities and strengths and should have unique missions. The body of Christ desperately needs this faithful, solid leadership contribution that rural churches have made over the years.

Much pastoral theology today centers on producing the "rancher"—the pastor who manages a large "spread." Although this ministry style seems up-to-date, it can be out of touch with the personal shepherding needs of the vast majority of congregations that actually exist. There are rapidly changing cultural situations everywhere, but they are not changing at the same speed or in the same direction. One-size-fits-all plans for ministry are no longer viable.

The "Country Shepherds' Workshop" of Oak Hills Fellowship is designed to train pastors wherever the traditional pastoral shepherding role is found. This book is the first of a series devoted to both affirming the value of pastorates in smaller settings and to making ministry methods culturally applicable in these settings. Our intent is not to write about things that *only* apply to rural churches but about things that definitely *will* apply there.

In *Growing Leaders by Design* Dr. Longenecker carefully demonstrates that Jesus had a plan for leadership development and that this plan is relevant for the church today. In this "how to" study, he shows us how a shepherd-type pastor can reproduce leaders. The intentional production of mid-level leadership in the church requires a personal nurturing beyond the concerns of ordinary discipleship.

Dr. Longenecker has ministered in a wide range of contexts—from Pennsylvania Dutch to rural southland to mid-west rural to mountain cowboy country to suburban Chicago to inner city Racine. He is a regular adjunct faculty member of the "Country Shepherds' Workshop." He is a wonderful teacher, a dedicated pastor, a voracious reader, and is always looking for people in other disciplines who think about issues that concern us. Yet for all this solid scholarship, you will find the strength of his writing is its faithfulness to the gospel record of the life of Jesus. May God use this publication for His glory in the church!

JOSEPH P. SMITH, Director
Church Ministries Department
Oak Hills Fellowship

Introduction

Like every kid growing up, I longed for worthy leadership models. There was the Lone Ranger, of course, but deep down I knew he wouldn't do. And there was "Big Jim," the almost perfect sixteen-year-old leader of Sugar Creek Gang fame. Both soon vanished, however, in the mists of unreality.

Then "Pastor John" came on the scene. Long before the term became popular, Pastor John Hiestand typified leadership excellence. He was a young. married man pastoring our little mission church, and I was able to watch him at work. Time and again I found myself saying, "If God ever calls me to be a pastor, I hope I can do it the way John does it."

John retired at age sixty-five and died at eighty-two. The tiny congregation he founded had grown to about a thousand people. Half again that many attended his visitation and funeral. Along with others, I shared in the memorial service. Sermons, testimonies, and private comments etched out the profile of this man, a real servant leader:

- a man of faith
- a man of honesty and transparency
- a man who loved and respected people
- a man who had vision

- a man who could lead without being a dictator
- a man who gave his disciples room to grow

I hope you are not surprised to learn that John, and those around him, not only led in the formation and growth of a major new congregation, but also mentored a wave of pastors, missionaries, educators, and lay people—a whole new generation of leaders.

God's Leadership Idea

Developing leaders who can relate to themselves and others as whole people is a uniquely Christian undertaking, for long before now, Jesus launched the original leadership revolution by nurturing a few ordinary people toward mature Christian relationships. If we take Scripture seriously, we will arrive at two key assumptions, to be fully supported as we go along: (a) each believer is a potential leader at one level or another; and (b) leaders are first developed, then discovered.[1]

Becoming this kind of leader today requires the formation of some radically new attitudes and behaviors that grow out of a "kneading" process much like the one Jesus used in training His disciples. Since the Gospel of Mark is written with such insight and detail, Jesus' model is most clearly visible in the writings of John Mark. With him as our guide we will watch the Master at work as He kneads a cluster of human spirits into flexible leadership personalities.

This unique preparation process is beautifully pictured in the book of Jeremiah, chapter 18, where we watch the potter at work. The potter begins with a lump of clay which he must carefully knead and prepare. In a similar way God prepares leaders through the use of qualified human instruments who knead them into malleable, useful material. We speak of these human instruments as disciplers and mentors. The Son of God became man and invested three years of His earthly life to knead lumps of (human) clay into leaders for His future church. It is important to note that Jesus didn't just look for leaders— He *shaped* and He *grew* them!

Today's World

Those who go through this kneading and shaping process, then and now, are marked by a few crucial leadership characteristics—one of which is the capacity for relationships. They are able to respect and influence those around them, not just because of a natural affinity, but through a work of the Spirit that cuts across all personality and temperament patterns. With a marked level of relational competence at the core of this Spirit-designed personhood, other characteristics follow such as:

- a commitment to growth
- a sense of vision
- an empowering influence
- an ability to lead

I found these characteristics clearly expressed in Pastor John and those he nurtured toward leadership, and I am recognizing these characteristics in the thinking and writing of many people—even those from a nonreligious perspective. These principles are timeless. As one writer put it, though tomorrow's leaders may still need their "bag of management skills," they will be ineffective unless they learn to relate to themselves and others as "whole people."[2] This is the key factor in today's leadership quest. At the deepest of all levels, this is what the ministry of Jesus was all about.

Focus on Mentoring

This is not just another "discipling" text. Discipling experts are well aware that the end result of Jesus' training ministry was the disciples' ability to lead. But they usually focus, quite narrowly, on the discipling *process.* My approach is different. While building on the process, I want to show *how leaders emerge from a biblical discipling/mentoring ministry and what they look like when they appear.* Material is freely drawn from the discipling arena, but my attention is sharply focused, and the emerging leader is always clearly targeted.

This is a book about the *mentoring process,* the pastor coming alongside the people in the church, loving them, encouraging them in personal Christian growth, helping them catch a vision of what God can do through them, and calling them to step forward into leadership positions. It is amazing what God does through a church and a pastor when these principles are practiced.

A new generation of effective leaders is urgently needed—
from pastors and elders to ushers and custodians! I realize that
today's high-decibel cry is for "first-level" leaders—the thinkers,
opinion makers, and pacesetters who can escort us into the
twenty-first century. But "second-level" leaders are also needed—
usable yet unsung pastors, elders, deacons, teachers, evange-
lists, musicians, missionaries, ushers—a vast company of
unknowns who are adept in securing the wholesome followership
of others.

To my knowledge, there is no *sure* way to intentionally grow
first-level leaders. But the Bible offers a way to intentionally
develop leaders at the second level. And if we work intelligently
at level two, who knows what wonderful fruit may eventually
be born at level one.

This book offers some basic insights as to how authentic Christian servant leaders can be brought along and made effective.
Specifically, it shows how

- you and I can become leaders,
- we can help others become leaders,
- the process can keep happening in our own circles, with
  people just like us.

Why did I write it? Because, from as far back as I can recall, I
have been intrigued with leaders and leadership. When Pastor
John became my model and my mentor, the blessings of his
loving encouragement triggered a curiosity about leadership that
continues to this day and yields insights that have proved applicable to all fields of Christian endeavor.

The book is designed for pastors and others who work with
leadership teams and trainees. I know how frustrating it is to
search for materials to help in our mentoring ministry. I hope
my book will help fill part of the void. With thirteen chapters
and questions for discussion, it is suitable for personal study or
specially selected small groups.

Since the pattern is biblical, it applies to leaders, agencies,
and churches of all sizes, but I write with a special urgency to
pastors and leaders of smaller churches. For you I have a deep
and abiding love. I have spent most of my life either pastoring
small churches or working in ministries directly in touch with
small churches. What I write will have special relevancy to you

and the work you do. I pray that your path will be brightened and your work made bountifully effective.

Scripture references are from the *New King James Version* (NKJV) unless otherwise noted.[3]

Endnotes

1. Douglas Sherman and William Hendricks, *Your Work Matters to God* (Colorado Springs, CO: NavPress, 1987), 245. See also Andrew T. LePeau, *Paths of Leadership* (Downers Grove, IL: InterVarsity Press, 1983), 11.

2. Perry Pascarella, *Industry Week's Guide to Tomorrow's Executive* (New York: Van Nostrand and Reinhold Co., 1981), cover. Max DePree, *Leadership Is an Art* (New York: Harper Books, 1990). See also David McKenna, *Power to Follow, Grace to Lead* (Irving, TX: Word, Inc., 1989), 129.

3. *The New King James Version.* Copyright © 1979, 1980, 1982, Thomas Nelson, Inc., Publishers.

Section One

Patterns in Conflict

Have you ever wondered about leadership and leaders? If so, you'll want to listen very carefully as Jesus warns His disciples away from the pattern of "Gentile" leadership (Mark 10). Here He draws a "line in the sand" between the laws of His kingdom and those of human society. Section 1 challenges us to hear these words with the same seriousness as His disciples heard them. To do this, we must be acquainted with two leadership patterns, one operating in society and one owned and blessed by Jesus Christ. When reading chapter 1, notice:

- how the secular pattern promotes distance between leaders and the people they're supposed to lead,

- the destructive characteristics of this secular leadership pattern,

- that contemporary leadership patterns in both the church and secular society have been fashioned by the history of corporate America in the twentieth century,

- that this pattern has had harmful effects on the church.

• 1 •

The Pattern of Society

A new vision of leadership is sorely needed. Whatever we're doing isn't working. Definitions of leadership abound, a sure sign that someone is wandering around in the dark. David McKenna sees leadership "at a crossroads." And Oswald Sanders wrote that even the church lacks the leadership it "so desperately" needs.

Our culture has generated many ideas about how people can become leaders, but getting from here to there has never been easy.

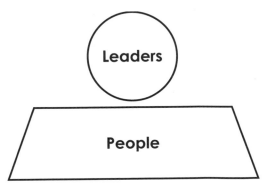

Figure 1

Destructive Characteristics

When I was a young man, I took a new job to support my growing family. "Joe," the main man in my department, always got the job done. As a combination bureaucrat and big-man leader, he loved his elite status and the perks that went with it. He played favorites, shunned interpersonal niceties, practiced "top down" management with gusto, treated workers as just another batch of materials, did what seemed right at the moment, and was judged a success because he got the job done.

Was it a terrible place to work? Not really. We workers often shared an enjoyable camaraderie (when Joe wasn't around), were not abused, and managed, on a very modest salary, to care for our families. But if someone had asked me how to go from "people" to "leader," I would have replied, "Pay your dues, keep your nose clean, and above all, get on Joe's good side."

While Joe's heavy-handed leadership pattern worked for him, there certainly are many other examples of good people who have brought dignity and grace to the secular workplace. In fact, the business community has many helpful things to teach us, like how to

- focus and delegate
- write mission statements
- develop purposes, objectives, and goals
- set priorities
- use technology

But along with all the good stuff, the corporate top-down model has saddled us with some destructive characteristics:

⬇ a leadership elite   ⬇

⬇ top–down control processes   ⬇

⬇ lack of respect for persons   ⬇

⬇ an ethic where ends justify the means   ⬇

⬇ leadership defined as an ability to do   ⬇

Figure 2

Secular Patterns

Where did these destructive characteristics come from? Out of the past century of corporate American history. At the risk of oversimplifying to the point of irrelevance, the 1900s can be divided into three time frames, each marked by a key perspective on leadership and management.[1]

Something I call Providence Leadership existed at the turn of the century. Translated, that means

Relish Your Inheritance

If you had it, you were gifted, blessed by God or nature, because leadership was a given. The inheritance could have been charisma, money, muscle, privilege, or position, which issued in a leadership validated by temperament, traits, personal "presence," physical prowess, or a sense of innate "power."[2]

The idea is with us yet. It has penetrated business, politics, and religion and has deeply affected evangelicalism. In the words of one highly placed, twentieth-century Christian leader, "When God wanted something done down through history, He chose a man, . . . placed him at the head of His people, and told them to follow and obey. . . . (So,) when he appears, follow him. Seek his vision, get his viewpoint, accept his plan. . . . One man must lead, many follow."[3]

However benign the intent, this is Providence Leadership. And it has enormous appeal. Imbued as we are with stories of priests and kings, prophets and apostles, we find it difficult to view leadership in other terms. After all, does God throw His treasures on the trash heap and limit Himself to the physically, emotionally, and intellectually crippled?

Of course not! But neither is He limited by innate endowments. God uses whom He pleases, great or small (1 Cor. 1:26). And though He can choose to use anyone, even some we might reject, His goal according to Mark 10:42–44 is to develop leaders who

- have the attitude of a servant,
- are committed to relationships,
- are submissive to the required training.

Providence Leadership won't do. But things change. During the 1920s a dramatic shift occurred in America's corporate life, and we were left with something that can be described as Positional Leadership, otherwise known as

Earn a Place in the Pecking Order

I refer to the modern bureaucracy that hit the country about 1925 and conditioned us to equate leadership with organizational position.

Under the influence of Max Webber, a psychologist from Germany, the bureaucratic "control" system became the wave of the future. Fredric Taylor, the "Father of Scientific Management," applied Webber's theories at General Motors, and *bureaucracy* was soon synonymous with *society*. Its purpose was to order relationships, businesses, governments, and cultures with machine-like efficiency.

The bureaucracy subtly instills the idea that leadership means gaining a position as a consequence of birth, appointment, or election. Everyone knows, of course, that position equals leadership. You're a nobody until you're a somebody. And to be a somebody, you need an appointment or an office.[4]

But once again, conventional wisdom is wrong. Though position and leadership often go together, one is not the other. It can easily turn out that position just equals position. Going to a mission field does not make a missionary, and gaining a position does not make a leader.

But there's more. After World War II, Process Leadership came along, which implies a need to

Master the Skills

We're talking about the management boom which spanned the decades of the fifties to the eighties. The management profession has fostered the idea that one is qualified to lead after learning how, after mastering the processes and meeting performance standards. So, the twentieth-century time line looks like this.

1900s	1920s	1950s	1990s

.. Providence .... Position .... Process .... (?) ....

Figure 3

Destructive Patterns in the Church

Do these patterns belong in the church? Not according to Jesus. Yet, the spirit and behaviors of the secular workplace are often found in the church in full bloom.

Some Christian leaders, like Joe, become "Mr. Strong Man." They rely on

- assets of birth or heritage
- strong natural endowments
- a charismatic temperament
- a divine call

Others become "Mr. Bureaucracy"

- in love with traditions
- officiously holding on to the old ways
- maintaining entrenched positions
- jealously guarding their fiefdoms

Still others end up being "Mr. Manager"

- applying all the sanctions
- task-centered and skills-oriented
- technology-driven
- focused only on getting the job done

Though Jesus warned of the danger of copying destructive secular patterns in Mark 10:42–44, we trip over these patterns again and again. As Christian leaders we have too often settled for the quick fix. Taking a firm grip on secular systems, we have wrapped them in Bible texts, sanctified them with religious terminology, and baptized them as Christian.

We're obviously relying on the wrong access routes. Taking our cues from secular society and the corporate workplace, we have adopted patterns that are out of sync with the principles of Scripture. A new vision of leadership is sorely needed, for most churches are full of ordinary Christians who want to make a difference in the work of God but aren't sure how to do it. Trying to cultivate biblical qualifications for leadership, they seem unsure of the process. Some who seem to be unqualified become leaders, even as others who appear qualified go nowhere.

After asking questions but getting few answers, Christians often conclude that leadership is gained by some mysterious providence or, more likely, by being "in" with the right people and playing politics. So, they give up.

From even this sketchy review, we learn that the destructive characteristics which plague our nation and our churches emerged from our corporate history. We also learn that, whether in or out of the church, those whose leadership is defined by one or another of these patterns tend to perpetuate

- a leadership elite
- top down controlling processes
- a view of workers as commodities
- an ethic where ends justify means
- leadership defined as an ability to perform

We're back to Mr. Strong Man, Mr. Bureaucracy, and Mr. Manager. Two results follow: "People" find it difficult to transition into the "Leaders" circle; and leadership development is reduced to "finding" them instead of "growing" them.

During the 1960s many Christian agencies found themselves organizationally deficient, so "Christian management" was shortly on the scene. It had its programs, literature, language, and leaders. Conferences during the sixties and seventies were incomplete without management seminars.

However we may assess the benefits of the movement (and there were many), the boom complicated efforts to define leadership. Whether ineptly vague or deliberately confusing, its vocabulary smudged the lines between leadership and management. Writers acknowledged that the two were different, but they were often scrunched together.[5]

This confusion resulted from the habit of subsuming leadership under the theme of management, the practice of most seminars and management manuals in the seventies, and thus leadership was denied a life of its own.[6] Thirty years of traditional management almost devoured the art of leadership.

Even more unsettling was the collateral idea that leadership is defined by technology, skills, or professionalism. Of course skills must be mastered if one is to lead, but one can master skills, functions, and processes and still lack the scriptural requirements for leadership.

But even as we scan the history, things keep changing. As traditional and participative management struggle in the workplace, the shape of the future remains uncertain. Only this is sure—change! But whatever happens, there is little doubt that the old deeply embedded patterns will continue to influence, covertly or overtly, how we lead and follow, in and out of the church. The concepts subconsciously determine how we think and live. They are sometimes present in almost undiluted form, sometimes adulterated, and sometimes mixed with a super-spiritual mind-set that allows the worst features of one or more patterns to plague God's people undetected, with terrible effect. And they are indiscriminately present in churches small and large.

But here's the shocker. If we do our homework, the three patterns finally merge into one: leadership competence is today largely gauged by an ability to "do leadership things." Whether derived from ancestry and privilege, from position, or from a knack for learning the ropes, one is ready to lead if one can do. This doing may mean almost anything:

- mastering leadership/management styles
- learning to be a "change agent"
- performing the functions of management
- just "doing what leaders do"[7]

If this assessment seems too harsh, listen to the comments of others:

> Samuel Escobar, writing in *The Evangelical Missions Quarterly*, sees the North American missions movement as gripped by a "managerial missiology," under a "task-oriented" perspective, with "technology and the social sciences" providing the "necessary methodologies."[8]

> Andrew LePeau says that our society has created technology and techniques and bowed down to them. And the church has "willingly followed the world's lead. . . ."[9]

> Glen T. Miller writes that the changes occurring in leadership training over the years have produced the "pragmatic professional." Knowledge has replaced virtue as the chief

qualification. "Those 'in the know' are those 'in the lead.'" Many even argue that only those with "know-how" should lead. As a result, leadership development is caught in a tug-of-war and the thing that is often missing is character.[10]

Some Christian bureaucrats have used their leadership positions as a covering for sin. Whereas in non-Christian groups these actions are frankly labeled as backstabbing, string-pulling, railroading, and dirty politics, in Christian groups the actions are often explained as being led by the Spirit, discerning God's will, or making decisions after much prayer.

A Call for Scriptural Leadership

Technology and the social sciences are not to be despised. But it is often implied that leaders are qualified just because they are skilled and can meet certain quantifiable performance levels. On this basis we may end up with a leadership grounded in human competencies, based on skills and abilities (inbred or acquired), and validated by sociology. Along the way, the molding of "lumps of clay" may be lost. Soberly considered, this should frighten us.

I understand the need for leaders to do leadership things. Out of forty years in the ministry, I spent thirteen as the senior pastor of multiple-staff churches and twenty-two as an administrator of church agencies. Of course we must be competent and comfortable with professional demands. But we must also be Christian, which means that we must first *be* something. And that leads us back to Jesus and the kneading process.

Don't expect the Joes of this world nor the patterns they espouse to quickly fade away. They are part of our culture. And we fail in our understanding of the current scene unless we realize that this is how things are. A massive misconception of how the church should be led characterizes today's thinking. Someone must call us back to the original pattern.

Is it possible that the small churches of America, under a new wave of dynamic pastors, could trigger this renewal? I believe so.

I've already said that the principles outlined here apply to all ministries, large or small. But leaders of megachurches, because of the size of their operations and a perceived need for quick decision making, are usually drawn toward the corporate model. For them, it seems to work! Though some leaders of large churches seek to honor biblical principles in their ministries, a full-scale return to the biblical pattern will not likely be led by the megachurch movement.

For the small church, the corporate pattern isn't an option. It isn't that pastors of smaller churches are more biblical or spiritual than their counterparts. The fact is, smaller churches do not typically respond well to the corporate model, and small church pastors, having no real alternative and out of sheer desperation, may be driven to the Bible for answers.

One more factor is worth mentioning. In the nature of things, the biblical leadership model and the small church form a unique fit. With little adaptation or experimentation, small church pastors can go seriously to work, with gratifying results.

Reflection/Discussion
1. How have the destructive characteristics of secular leadership patterns had an impact on *your* life? Make a list.
2. Have your thoughts and behaviors about leadership been affected? How? Discuss with someone else.
3. Identify some negative effects in the church.

Endnotes
1. Murry Ross and Charles Hendry, *New Understandings in Leadership* (New York: Associated Press, 1957), 13–31; Harry Levinsen, *The Exceptional Executive* (New York: Mentor Books, 1968), 156–57; Brian Hall and Helen Thompson, consulting author William Zierdt, *Leadership Through Values* (Ramsey, NJ: Paulist Press, 1980), 15.

2. E.T. Hollander, *Leaders, Groups and Influence* (New York: Oxford University Press, 1964), 4.

3. J. Oswald Smith, published in Missionary Tech Team newsletter, Longview, Texas. Original source not cited.

4. Morris Bogard, *The Managers Style Book* (Englewood Cliffs, NJ: Prentice-Hall, 1980), 106; Richard Wolff, *Man at the Top* (Wheaton IL: Tyndale House, 1970), 6.

5. Kenneth Gangel, *Competent to Lead* (Chicago: Moody Press, 1974), 73.

6. Campus Crusade for Christ, *Management Manual*, 1977.

7. Paul Hersey, *The Situational Leader* (New York: Warner Books, 1984); Lyle E. Shaller, *The Change Agent* (Nashville:

Abingdon Press, 1972); Jay E. Adams, *Pastoral Leadership:* (Grand Rapids: Baker), 13,14, entire book currently available in *Shepherding God's Flock* (Grand Rapids: Zondervan, 1986); Ted W. Engstrom and Edward R. Dayton, *The Art of Management for Christian Leaders* (Irving, TX: Word Inc., 1982).

8. Samuel Escobar, *Evangelical Missions Quarterly* (January 1991).

9. LePeau, *Paths of Leadership.*

10. Glen T. Miller, *Faith and Mission Magazine* (January, 1992). Some quotes taken from review in *Bibliotheca Sacra.*

Jesus' pattern of leadership is often talked about but rarely explained. In chapter 2 we seek to understand and apply His pattern. Drawn from the Gospels, it is in sharp contrast to the pattern around us and is a prototype of the best leadership insights history can offer. The pattern of Jesus transcends all others. At each step along the way, His words and example excel. When reading this chapter, notice:

- the emphasis in the Gospel of Mark on Jesus' ministry with His disciples;

- the clarity of Jesus' pattern in the Gospel of Mark;

- the contrast between Figures 1 and 4;

- the importance of community;

- the interplay between group mentoring and personal discipling.

• 2 •

The Pattern of Jesus

The ministry of *leadership mentoring*, when viewed through the grid of intentional leadership development, takes on some new and exciting hues.[1] A fresh look at the methods of Jesus is therefore in order. Through the eyes of John Mark

- we watch as Jesus applies the principles.
- we observe leaders emerging from the process.
- we identify their key characteristics.

Let's begin with the principles Jesus used.

Servant Leadership

Pastor John was a servant. He was also professionally competent. But servanthood was never sacrificed on the altar of professionalism. The words of Jesus were lived out:

> You know that those who are considered rulers over the Gentiles lord it over them, and their great ones exercise authority over them. Yet it shall not be so among you . . . whoever desires to become great among you shall be your servant. And whoever of you desires to be first shall be slave of all (Mark 10:42–44).

Note the words "lord over" and "authority over." Whether it is

27

some variety of leadership elitism, office holding, or management expertise, the end result is often a form of domination and control. By contrast, it is the spirit of a servant, expressed in personal example, that defines the heart of Christian leadership.

In the words of Philip Greenslade, Jesus "expressly repudiates every secular mode. . . . No category, whether social, cultural, ecclesiastical, or political will fit His vision . . . without drastic alteration in style and attitude." [2]

D. E. Hoste, successor to Hudson Taylor, said that when a man, by virtue of an official position in the church, "demands the obedience of another, irrespective of the latter's reason and conscience, this is the spirit of tyranny. When, on the other hand, . . . (he) is able *to influence and enlighten another so that the latter, through the medium of his own reason and conscience, is led to alter one course or adopt another, that is true spiritual leadership.*" [3] (italics mine)

Leaders of this caliber can

* have authority yet not abuse it,
* hold an office yet stand above the bureaucracy,
* use management skills yet remain sensitive.

They treat people well, not for utilitarian purposes but because to do so is to act righteously. And people follow them because their leadership has been earned.

But where do servant leaders come from? Are they just there as part of the landscape? Or are they developed?

The Source

Servant leaders are not just there, waiting to be picked. They require a suitable climate in which to grow and mature, and it is the task of Christian leaders to help create that climate. A church or group that creates a climate in which God's people can become all that His grace can make them will inevitably grow leaders.

The level of leadership at which the person functions will be affected by many factors—temperament, innate talents, education, experience, spiritual gifts, the call of God, diligence—none of which is my concern at present. But this is certain—*a conducive climate will bring forth leaders.* While some potential leaders will fall short of their possibilities, we will be amazed at those who come forth and move out, many whom we would never have imagined.

Embedded in the Gospels

The Gospels reveal how the incarnate God came to earth to train future leaders in His church. Jesus confirmed His work as a maker of leaders when He prayed, "I have finished the work You gave me to do" (John 17:4). As Leroy Eims says in *The Lost Art of Disciple Making,* Jesus was speaking primarily of His "men." "Forty times He refers to the 'men' whom the Father had given Him out of the world. These men were His work. . . . He gave His life on the cross for millions, but during the . . . years of His earthly ministry, He gave Himself uniquely to these men."[4]

Read the Gospels carefully, and the story leaps right out at you. The planting of His church in the world required the training of this little group for leadership in that church.

Revealed in Mark

Mark offers unique insights into the training ministry of Jesus. Dr. Robert Meye points out that it was the disciples and not the crowds that were central to Mark's story; that Jesus' offer to make them "fishers of men" was His assurance that they would one day have a ministry like His; that His pre-Easter promise to meet them in Galilee after the resurrection is a signal that the disciples' band would be reformed in the very place their discipleship had begun (14:28); that the coming of the Spirit would climax their preparation.[5]

More to our point, however, is Meye's central conclusion that Jesus planned His training work in steps or stages, leading His men "from one level of understanding to another." He identifies four such stages:

1. From their call to their apostolic appointment
2. From their appointment to Caesarea-Philippi
3. From Caesarea-Philippi to Jerusalem
4. From Jerusalem to Pentecost [6]

In section 2 of this book we walk through these four stages and notice what happens as the disciples go through the "kneading" process.

Inaugurated with the Twelve

If Jesus' aim was to turn in a quick, flashy success story, He chose a strange batch of disciples. The "before" picture is anything but encouraging. These men held no synagogue seats, nor were they priests. They were just common laboring men and by any standard of sophisticated culture would surely be considered a rather ragged bunch. A. B. Bruce sees them as "ignorant, narrow-minded, superstitious, full of Jewish prejudices, misconceptions, and animosities."[7]

But how different they appear "after." Now Bruce honors them as "enlightened of mind and endowed with charity." And though they were far from perfect, they were men of such "excellent moral stuff" that having been so long with Jesus, they would prove to be "good and noble men when they came before the world as leaders."

What happened to these fellows between the "before" and the "after"? Change! That's what happened—dramatic change! They grew toward maturity, toward personal and spiritual whole-ness, toward Spirit-controlled personhood, which translates into a capacity to lead. Mark puts the final touch to his story as he pens the last sentence of his gospel. These men, formerly "igno-rant" and "narrow minded," full of "prejudices, misconceptions, and animosities" were now qualified to evangelize the world, to preach the Gospel "everywhere."[8]

Except for Judas, this change was true of them all. The picture of the disciples sitting idly in Jerusalem while others evan-gelized does not fit all the facts. According to Acts 8:1, this hesitation may have been the case for one brief point, but evidence strongly suggests that the twelve disciples did indeed go everywhere, telling Christ's message and planting His church.[9] It was not Luke's purpose to record the whole story of the early church, but to touch those events that charted the Gospel's progress from Jerusalem to Rome.

The Method of Jesus

The only realistic explanation for this change in the disciples is the pattern of personal transformation employed by the Savior. The facts are incredibly simple.

1. Jesus called.
2. His men followed.

3. They lived with Him.
4. They became leaders
5. They trained others.

This feat was not achieved because Jesus waved a magic wand nor was it the result of one mighty miraculous act. He reached His goal by employing a few powerful approaches that are available to His followers in any age. The graph below, reflecting this unique pattern, contrasts dramatically with that of society.

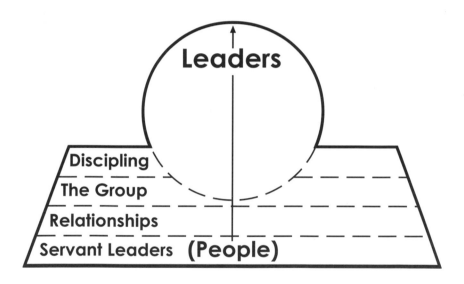

Figure 4

The pattern of Jesus, fashioned from a blend of four dynamic elements, creates a unique and powerful approach to the ministry of leadership development.[10] Here we see the approach Jesus followed to grow *leaders* for His church out of *ordinary people*.

The Servant Leader

Jesus Himself, the archetype servant leader, illustrates the crucial truth that without credible servant leaders as models, we have no worthy pattern. *To end up with servant leaders, we must begin with them.* Thank God, there are always a few to be found. But just because a leader is "successful" is no guarantee that he is a true servant. For good or ill, leaders reproduce after their own kind. To end up with servant leaders, we must begin with servant leaders.

The Relationship

Jesus also formed relationships. When He appointed the Twelve to their apostleship, He instructed them, first of all, to "be with Him." And of course, like spokes on a wheel, to be with Him meant that they would also be with each other.

What do we mean by relationships? Surely not just the warm fuzzies. Christian relationships should be marked by honest, forthright dealing with one another, as we really are, as we are before God, and beyond the level of polite appearance.

Francis Schaeffer has said that unless the church changes its forms and gets back to community and the sharing of lives personally, the church is done.

And according to Larry Richards, love is communicated only when relationships are close enough for the reality of love to be experienced.

Why should relationships matter? Because our ministries are poorly done if relationships are out of order. To *minister* means to preach, teach, counsel, comfort, disciple, confront, administer, and much more! But if relationships are messy,

- preaching and teaching are deadened
- comfort is deflected
- discipling and mentoring are dulled
- discipline is derailed
- administration is desensitized

The demands of the ministry require the leader-in-process to be exposed to vital, authentic relationships on the way to becoming a leader. Any program that ignores this factor is inadequate and even suspect.

The Bonded Group

The group matters for ever so many reasons, but above all else, it is the key to personal and emotional maturity. A small group offers the best hope for personal change. In the community of Christ we become free, free enough, and safe enough, for our unique traits to develop and that which has been tied up along the way is allowed to emerge.

Certain key growth steps are more likely to occur in groups than in one-on-one interactions. While leading a graduate level class, I monitored a group of pastoral students involved in peer interaction on class projects. "Bill," who pastored in a rural cultural context, was reared in a large city. Both pastor and people were being pushed way beyond their comfort zones. His class project was designed to locate the reasons why people were slow to accept him, then chart an appropriate response. One answer was obvious. Though Bill was sincere and dedicated, he looked and acted like what he was, a man from the city. But he was serving among decidedly noncity people.

The students listened carefully as Bill explained his project. As data was given, shared, and received, the discussion moved toward closure. Just then "Sam," older and wiser, raised a penetrating question: "But what are your people afraid of?" And Bill answered, "That some 'city slicker' will mess up their church." The ensuing silence echoed and re-echoed with Sam's measured response: "It seems to me that your people's worst fears have come upon them."

Did Bill grow through that exchange? Indeed, all of us did. I watched in awe as each person was ministered to, even as they ministered. No individual alone could have produced that result. Bill grew in an awareness of the issues separating him and his people, and in personal maturity. And all of us learned something new about how God works among us.

When we build groups (small groups in larger churches or whole congregations in smaller churches), we build community.

Jesus, too, relied on community, on the group. His men learned to relate to and profit from each other. Their cohesiveness was an element in their training. We learn the same way. It is only in the community of faith that we can become whole persons, learning to accept ourselves and extend acceptance to others.

When attempting to grow leaders, don't forget the group. It's a key part of the climate.

The Discipling Method

The final approach is discipling. Scriptural discipling exerts a power that is, even now, gravely undervalued. Support for this claim comes from an unusual source, Albert Bandura of Stanford University. Using the terms "behavior modification" and "imitative learning," he illustrates, through personal research, the contrast between what we might describe as professional instruction and mentoring. He explains that behavioral modification requires us to learn by doing, failing, and doing again under the competent professional. On the other hand, imitative learning happens under the influence of long association with a few significant and admired persons.

As a result of imitative learning, Bandura says, we acquire "large, integrated patterns of behavior," without having to form them by "tedious trial and error" methods. He concludes that we "learn most from those we regularly associate with, and from those we admire." [11]

Since imitative learning is obviously the equivalent term for discipling or mentoring, we may conclude that "large, integrated patterns of behavior" (values, principles, wisdom, insight) are imparted by discipling/mentoring. Suddenly a unique contrast emerges between the effects of the *group,* and the effects of more personal *mentoring: the group builds personhood, while mentoring builds character.*

Why, then, is there so much indifference toward imitative learning? Bandura blames the scientists who are so preoccupied with behavioral modification that they ignore the alternative. He cites a current and popular psychology text that uses twenty pages to discuss behavioral modification, assigning two for imitative learning. Unfortunately, the Christian community has once again learned the wrong lessons all too well.

Ron Lee Davis, in *Mentoring: Strategy of the Master,* has done us a great service by portraying a discipling dimension that is often missed. Rather than another program in which someone called a "discipler" schedules regular meetings with a key "disciple" to transfer content from one head to another, *discipling is a relationship and a lifestyle.* Jesus relied on a daily ministration of nurturing. His men changed because He loved them, lived among them, shared Himself with them, taught them, and put up with them. As a result, people found out what it meant to "be with Jesus" (Acts 4:13). [12]

Conclusion

While readers may differ with some specifics, the conceptual underpinnings of this chapter are, I think, biblically validated. They rest on the record of the Gospels, and as we shall see, on the testimony of the Epistles as well. Moreover, we could compile a large bibliography that would undergird what is here outlined, namely that Jesus called and developed twelve men for the purpose of becoming the leaders of His church. Since they were by no means intrinsic leaders when He found them, it is clear that He developed them. He painstakingly performed this work, over a period of three years, by using Himself as a worthy model, building relationships, and fostering the group, so that He could mentor them to leadership maturity. Moreover, the evidence suggests that we are called to do the same kind of work, using His pattern.

Obviously, we are not Jesus. As we disciple/mentor others, we point them ultimately to Jesus Christ, saying with Paul, "Follow me, as I follow Christ" (Phil. 3:12, 17). We realize, too, the need for dependence on the Holy Spirit who indwells and empowers the mentor, as well as energizing and leading the one being mentored. We also understand the need to be involved with the body of Christ, to avoid going it alone. But with these qualifications, the pattern stands. It is defensible, and it works.

Why, then, is the task so seldom undertaken or pursued with such little dedication and enthusiasm? I think the answer must be that the work is hard, demanding, and costly. And in addition to not knowing how, we are perhaps unwilling to pay the price, for to do this work requires:

1. A willingness to invest in long-term, authentic relationships, and that's not easy;
2. A commitment to modeling, which is not only hard, but often embarrassing. It demands a level of honesty that can be intimidating and even frightening;
3. An investment of time—time for individual persons and time for our efforts to produce results—usually involving a period of years.

Almost everything connected with current ministry patterns is incompatible with this focus. Shallow relationships are the norm, vulnerability is shunned, and time is at a premium. If the work is ever to be done, a reorientation of thinking and practice must take place. But we can do this work, right now, in today's world, as we carry on our pastoral ministries. The elements are simple! Demanding, but simple! We start by becoming

- authentic servant leaders,
- who form relationships,
- create community by building groups,
- so we can mentor others toward leadership.

We have the resources. It is only required that we use them.

Reflection/Discussion
1. In your own words, state the difference between the patterns of society and the pattern of Jesus.
2. Reflect on the four components of Jesus' leadership development pattern and discuss these the following questions with another person. Why is the leader so important? Explain the value of relationships. What does the group contribute? Why is discipling crucial?
3. Foster your own climate of development. Get in touch with a servant leader and allow him to impact your life. List the person(s) with whom you have developed a relationship that is more than casual. Become part of a bonded group—Sunday school class, growth group, support group, or informal prayer/study group.

Endnotes
1. My theme is *leadership* discipling, not just *discipling.* More precisely, it is *leadership mentoring.* If you want specialized discipling instruction, read Bill Hull, *The Disciple-Making Pastor* and *The Disciple-Making Church* (Tarrytown, NY: Fleming H. Revell, 1988).

2. Philip Greenslade, *Leadership, Greatness, and Servanthood* (Minneapolis: Bethany House Publishers, 1984), 2–3.

3. D.E. Hoste, *If I Am to Lead* (Littleton, CO: OMF Books, 1968).

4. Leroy Eims, *The Lost Art of Disciple Making* (Grand Rapids: Zondervan, 1978).

5. Robert Meye, *Jesus and the Twelve: Discipleship and Revelation in Mark's Gospel* (Grand Rapids: Eerdmans, 1968);

Ray Stedman, *The Servant Who Rules* (Irving, TX: Word, Inc., 1976); Kent Tucker, "Principles of Discipleship in the Training of the Twelve in Mark's Gospel," master's thesis, Dallas Theological Seminary; Herman Harrell Horne, *Teaching Techniques of Jesus* (Grand Rapids: Kregel Publications, 1971).

6. Meye's work beautifully confirms the four stages of Jesus' discipling ministry (see section 2).

7. A. B. Bruce, *The Training of the Twelve* (Grand Rapids: Kregel, 1971), 14.

8. See comments on page 68, and notes 1–2 on page 70 for the explanation regarding the manuscript genuineness of Mark 16:9–20 and related questions.

9. William Stuart McBirnie, *Search for the Twelve Apostles* (Wheaton, IL: Tyndale, 1975); Paul L. Maier, *In the Fullness of Time* (New York: Harper, 1991), 335–37.

10. Note the following differences between Figures 1 and 4.
  a. In Fig. 4, the "leaders" circle, partly within the "people" foundation, illustrates identity.
  b. The dotted line between the foundation and the "leader" circle (Fig. 4) shows ease of movement from one to the other.
  c. The dotted lines (Fig. 4) between the foundation elements show the components flowing cohesively together as servant leaders and emerging leaders share a network of relationships in one or more groups.

11. Albert Bandura, quoted in Robert H. Watermann Jr., *The Renewal Factor* (New York: Bantam Books, 1987), 4–5.

12. Ron Lee Davis, *Mentoring: Strategy of the Master* (Chicago: Moody Press, 1991).

Section Two

The Pattern of Jesus Applied to the Disciples

Jesus' leadership pattern is visible in all the Gospels, but in Mark it takes on a very special clarity. In section 2 we follow as Mark leads us through the ministry of Jesus with His disciples. Chapter headings are my own, though I thank Dr. Meye for confirming the view that the process goes through four sequential stages. The chapters expound the stages, showing how Jesus uses each stage to transfer a key quality of leadership to His men. And since faith is the foundation of leadership, He begins by leading His men to believe. When reading this chapter, notice:

- Jesus' ministry is timeless in its application,

- the nature of faith,

- faith must be alive,

- the correlation between believing and leading,

- if we choose to lead, it is first necessary to believe.

• 3 •

Leading Them to Believe

When is a Christian ready to lead? What credentials do we look for? Natural abilities? "Spirituality"? Leadership traits? Academic degrees? Giftedness? Skills? And why were the disciples qualified to lead? Because under the greatest leader-maker in history, they grew toward mature Christian personhood. Their unique pilgrimage—from impotence to influence, from mediocrity to excellence, from obscurity to prominence—began when they were touched by the training ministry of Jesus. And in every life that gives birth to leadership, a similar process seems to occur.

Fred Rogers (of *Mr. Rogers' Neighborhood* fame) tells college graduates to reach out and touch others. He believes that anyone who lives life with any degree of competence "has had at least one person, and often many, who have believed in him or her." We don't get to be competent people "without a lot of different investments from others."

Or consider the story of author Phillip Keller. When he was only eight years of age, his missionary parents sent him to a "gaunt, gloomy" boarding school, with its "gongs, bells, whistles" and the "barked commands" of instructors. But one person, "by her quiet, strong love," saved him from ruin. She was a "tiny, hunchbacked, plain woman," with "no idea how to dress charmingly," yet she lived a life that radiated the love of Christ. She

41

sensed Keller's "aloneness" and "gently came alongside" to "let him get a glimpse of Christ" in her life. On one occasion Phillip heard her tell his parents, "You may not believe it now but one day God will use this lad of yours to achieve great things for His honor." And from that moment, Keller "believed it could happen."[1]

Four Training Stages

Consciously or unconsciously, under mentors prominent or obscure, through contacts formal or informal—it happens. Scratch a servant leader and you'll find one or more episodes of intensive growth triggered by mentors who developed relationships, fostered groups, nurtured people to maturity, and turned them into *becomers.*

For a profile of emerging servant leaders, read Mark's gospel. Trace out the sequences of Jesus' ministry with the Twelve, and a picture gradually appears. They are people of *faith,* in a *process of growth, learning to relate, envisioning the future.* For Jesus, the training was conscious and intentional and achieved through four training stages. During these stages He transferred the qualities of faith, growth, relational competence, and vision.

- In Mark 1:1–3:19, He reproduces a Living Faith
- In Mark 3:19–9:29, He reproduces Dynamic Growth
- In Mark 9:30–10:52, He reproduces Relational Competence
- In Mark 11:1–16:20, He reproduces Vision

Change the nouns into participles and you have people who are prepared to lead, the "becomers"—*believing, growing, relating, aspiring*—leaders in process! Not finished, still becoming, but on the way and increasingly marked by character, conviction, godliness, mature personhood, vision, and influence.

Background to Faith

Since the whole process hinges on believing, Jesus begins with faith. He calls twelve men to be His disciples. His call is set against the backdrop of an amazing ministry.

- He came preaching in Galilee (1:14)
- He came teaching in the synagogue (1:22)

- He came in power, delivering from demons (1:23)
- He came praying, alone (1:35)
- He healed Peter's mother-in-law (1:29)
- He healed the multitudes (1:32)
- He even healed lepers (1:40)
- He healed a cripple (2:1–12)
- He also forgave the man's sins (2:1–12)
- He met the religious consensus head on (2:18–3:6)

He did all this with a spirit of gracious compassion. Mark paints a vivid picture of Jesus—coming, serving, preaching, teaching, and allowing Himself to be seen and heard and known. And as we call people to faith in Jesus Christ, we can point to the same magnificent ministry as proof that His claims are valid.

Call to Faith

John recounts an early episode when two disciples of John the Baptist, meeting Jesus, asked where He was staying (John 1:35–42). "Come and see," He answered. And they did! Jesus could be known, touched, observed, a fact John didn't forget when he wrote, "that which was from the beginning, which we have seen and heard, . . . and our hands have handled concerning the Word of Life, . . . we declare unto you" (1 John 1:1–3).

In the climate of that personal exposure the Savior called His men, by ones and twos, until He had twelve. Mark tells of the call of only five. He saw Peter and Andrew casting their nets and cried out, Come, and they followed (Mark 1:16–18). He went a few steps down the beach and saw James and John mending their nets. They followed too! (Mark 1:19–20) Later he passed the office of a tax collector and called a fellow named Matthew (Levi). He, too, came along (Mark 2:14).

A few were followers of Jesus before their formal call. But the drama is arresting. One moment they were going about their business, and the next they were disciples of Jesus. The pattern was always the same. "Come after me," said Jesus, and they came! And having gathered His men together, He called them to a mountain top where He appointed them to their apostleship (Mark 3:14).

And one thing more! Luke 6:12 suggests that this One who came praying, spent a night alone in prayer before appointing His men to their apostolic office. Thus, the call occurred in a context of intercession. On the basis of John 17, I suggest that Jesus prayed often and regularly for His men. And may God help us to learn that the development of leaders requires mentors who pray.

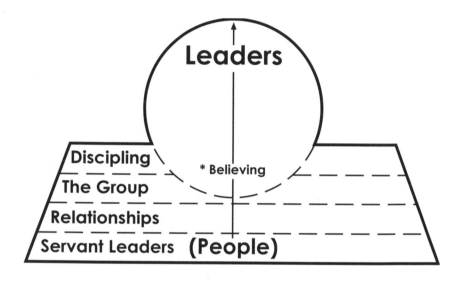

Figure 5

Men of Faith

By His choice and their commitment, they were men of faith. The first quality of leadership has been transferred. They were now believing people. They believed the faith, and their faith was alive.

But what is faith? Great thinkers and writers such as Tolstoy have said that "to believe is as essential as air and water." Emerson wrote that "a man bears belief as a tree bears apples." Pascal wrote that it is "natural for the mind to believe."

Mark McCloskey, writing in *Tell It Often, Tell It Well,* says that people are equipped with a God-given desire to find an object, person, or cause to serve and worship. He concludes that *faith is "the act of placing one's trust in an object considered worthy of one's allegiance and service."*[2] This is precisely what the disciples did.

Why it is that some make that faith-response while others do not is an issue we leave unaddressed. It is enough to say that little progress will be made until a person is willing to say "Lord, I choose to be your disciple." The key is availability.

In *Disciples are Made—Not Born*, William Henrichsen tells of a Navigator staff member who had formerly worked for a banana company in his home town of Kingston, Jamaica. One day an executive commended him for his work and assured him of a fine future. "But I warn you," said the agent, "you must give your life in exchange for bananas." As the disciples chose Jesus in place of fish, the young man chose Christ instead of bananas.

Priority of Faith

First, *faith is the fountainhead of values and morals.* Many secular experts are speaking out about the need for leaders with "values." The source of these values, however, is rarely specified. But those who understand historic Christianity realize that values derive from faith. At a more personal level, any quest after true godliness is doomed unless is rests on a faith commitment to Jesus Christ and His Word.

Faith is also important because *it triggers personal and spiritual Christian growth.* Since I will have a good deal to say later on about the need for leaders to grow, to change, to become everything God's grace can make them, it is worth noting that secular writers are deeply into the same theme. But apart from a biblical faith foundation, they lack an agreed-upon starting point, a goal toward which to move, and a sure way of getting there.

Then, too, faith is crucial because *it is the matrix for relational competence.* The relational dimensions of biblical faith suggest that Christian experience lacks authenticity unless one is in the process of becoming relationally competent. An "isolated Christian" is a contradiction in terms.

Finally, without a vital faith, *progress toward a wholesome and church-strengthening vision is limited.* Coming up with a batch of visions isn't difficult. But fashioning a God-honoring and stable *sense* of vision that will influence the people of God to follow godly leaders drives us back to our starting point.

Conclusion

For the disciples, their faith commitment was the first step in becoming leaders. Though their perception of Jesus was not as clear as it would eventually become, they were gripped by a faith that survived even though greatly tested (John 6:68). It not only survived, it became progressively more dynamic.

We can transmit that same kind of faith to others. Introduce a friend to the Savior, root his faith in Jesus Christ, lead him to an act of commitment, ground him in the Word, and you reproduce a living faith—a faith that allows God free access into his life and stimulates him to do serious business with God.

That's the critical issue. Does our faith drive us to know God, to open our lives to Him, to be in touch with Him—through His Word, through prayer, and through fellowship in Christ's body? If so, the foundation is laid for the next stage. Otherwise, we need to look again to the foundation.

Reflection/Discussion
1. Read the references in the "background" paragraph on pp. 42–43. How can Jesus' ministry call forth faith today?
2. List the elements of the Gospel (1 Cor. 15:1–4).
3. Describe your own faith to yourself and then to someone else.

Endnotes
1. Mark McCloskey, *Tell It Often, Tell It Well* (San Bernardino, CA: Here's Life Publishers, 1990), 91.
2. Ibid.

Newborn babies and newborn believers must grow. But healthy growth requires a healthy climate. To grow toward spiritual maturity calls for a climate of acceptance, love, honesty, accountability, and freedom to become all that God's grace can make us. How appropriate that as we come to the next stage of the process, Jesus has just such a climate ready for the disciples. And as He led them to "believe," He now helps them to "grow." When reading this chapter, notice:

- the "heart" of the growth climate,

- the disciples' growth experiences,

- the value of pain,

- that faith precedes growth,

- that dynamic growth is experienced by all who lead well.

• 4 •

Helping Them to Grow

Every family, someone has said, tattoos its children while still in the cradle with the traditions of the tribe. Jesus, too, stitched the new-found faith of His disciples to an experience of growth that, little by little, formed them into His own image. But contrary to secular society that tries to change us on the *outside*, Christ goes about the task of helping us grow and making us new from the *inside* as He works "on the thinking, the attitudes, the values and the character" of those who aspire to lead.[1] Christian leaders must *grow* as well as *believe,* for static, plastic, half-people cannot effectively lead others.

No one can be forced to grow. But Sherman and Hendricks say, and rightly so, that growth to effective leadership is an option for everyone.

Climate for Growth (Mark 3:14)
When Jesus set His disciples apart for their apostleship, He stressed that they were to "be with Him" (Mark 3:14). Note that phrase! They would preach later, but first they would be with Him. Jesus was launching a history-making project. He needed men whom He could release to the world as leaders (Eph. 2:20). Hence, *their first task was to be with Him and become like Him.*

The disciples soon discovered what this companionship meant. As Jesus taught in a little house in Galilee, those standing by

49

the door announced that His mother and brothers were seeking Him. "Who are My mother and My brothers?" asked Jesus (Mark 3:31–35). Sweeping the circle with a glance and pausing to gaze on the disciples, He answered, "Here are My mother and My brothers." And Matthew says that as He spoke, Jesus "stretched His hand toward the disciples" (Matt. 12:49).

This episode reflects no disrespect for Jesus' kinfolk, but it reminds us that His relationships with the Twelve were intensely serious. This early event is just a foretaste, a promise, of the love that would be more dramatically shown as Jesus' ministry drew to a close (John 13:1).

Vibrant growth does not happen in cold, sterile settings. But the circle Jesus formed in which the disciples lived and moved was honest, warm, accepting, supportive, even confrontive—and prayerful. It called for accountability but offered immeasurable blessings in return.

So, the disciples grew! As Jesus "opened the understanding" of two followers after His resurrection (Luke 24:25), He now "opens" His men, in a more elemental way, to His life-changing ministry.

Dimensions of Growth (Mark 3:19–9:29)

Mark 3:19 to 9:29 gives us an excellent picture of the growth of the disciples in their intellect, experience, emotions, spirit, and ministry skills.

They grew conceptually through private tutoring (4:10, 34; 7:17; 8:15). Once and again Jesus turns from the crowds to share special insights with His men, to more carefully explain the truth He had given others. He knew the minds of His men needed enlarging, needed a firm grip on the truth. Though their intellectual equipment varied greatly, He would not allow them to be sluggish. Though it hurt, He made them think.

They grew experientially as they shared dramatic glimpses of His glory. In chapter 5, Peter, James, and John went with Him to heal the daughter of Jairus. In chapter 6 He appeared to His men on the sea as they rowed valiantly to reach shore. Chapter 9 reveals the magnificence of the Transfiguration. These events taught the disciples that following Jesus was a rousing adventure.

They grew emotionally as He opened Himself to them at deep emotional levels. Imagine being there as He is rejected in His home town. "A prophet is not without honor," He says, "except in his own country and among his own kin and in his own house." Hear Him as He speaks and watch a deep sadness settle over His face (6:1–6). Was ever a mentor more vulnerable, more ready to let His pain be seen? And could these men share His hurt without enlarging their own ability to feel personal pain?

They grew spiritually as He led them to confess His deity at Ceasarea Phillippi. Peter spoke for them all when he said, "You are the Christ, the Son of the Living God" (Matt. 16:16). Peter's profession stands as an ultimate witness to the revealing and illuminating work of the Spirit of God.

They grew practically as He taught them to serve others (6:7–3). They went out at His command—preaching, healing, and casting out devils. They were doing what He promised. At the end their tour (6:30–31), the Lord led them away for a time of rest, which no doubt included an evaluation session. They would surely do it better the next time.

Understand that the disciples were not yet grown—just growing. Even so, they began to express characteristics that all of us long to see in young believers—love for the Lord, hunger for His Word, an interest in prayer, and a passion for progress, though their aspirations were sometimes distorted.

As a result of this stretching process, they found themselves kneaded and shaped by totally new experiences. Just a few months ago they were catching fish and swapping stories with their fishing buddies, collecting taxes, and sharing the latest synagogue gossip. Now they are preaching, casting out demons, teaching, and healing. They were launched on a growth trajectory that would leave them forever different from what they once were.

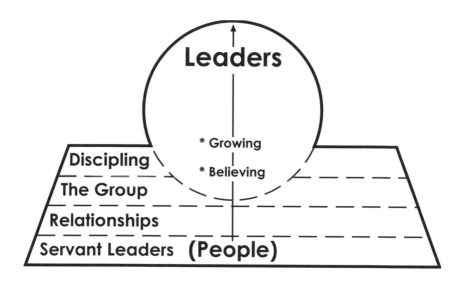

Figure 6

Formula for Growth

Paul Tournier compares the experience of growth to learning how to perform on the trapeze. You hang onto a bar for dear life, knowing that unless you let go and grasp another, you're stuck. So, growth has its risk, change inspires fear, and risk and change spell pain—which puts us at the heart of Jesus' growth formula:

- recurring sequences of elation, risk, and pain,
- in vital fellowship with other strugglers,
- under the guidance of His authoritative Word,
- sustained by His presence and His disciplines.

Think of the disciples as they watched the miracles, sensed the hatred of the religious leaders, shared the rejection of Jesus at Nazareth, ventured on their ministry tour, heard of the death of John the Baptist, marveled over the feeding of the multitude, and experienced the Transfiguration. Each event had its quota of joy and pain.

One of these events, the miracle of the loaves and fishes, stands out above all others for risk, pain, joy, and growth potential. It did more to shock these men into at least a semiconscious spiritual state than any previous experience.

You recall that this is the only miracle recorded by all four Gospels. Furthermore, it came at the climax of Jesus' Galilean ministry and marked the beginning of that ministry's decline. If we sift carefully through the four accounts of this event, we are left with several serious implications—for the Jews, for Jesus, and especially for the disciples.

Consider the disciples' state of mind as they return from a ministry tour and find their weekend retreat ruined by an insensitive crowd that precipitated

> an unplanned desert preaching mission . . . a command to feed the people . . . Andrew finding a little boy with some food . . . the miracle . . . a mysterious trip across the sea as Jesus prays alone . . . the storm . . . Jesus' ghostly night-time appearance . . . a killer sea instantly calmed . . . the sermon the next day on the "bread of life" . . . a bruising conflict with the religious hierarchy . . . the massive defection of His followers . . . a troubling question for His men: "Do you also want to go away?" (Mark 6:30–56; John 6:67).

For the disciples, this was a pain-filled forty-eight hours. They came face-to-face with unsettling questions about the One they had chosen to follow. From a human perspective, a strange batch of facts demanded attention. It looked very much as though this One to whom they had given their allegiance had senselessly put them through a two-day spiritual meat grinder.

Very strange, even frightening! And yet, there were those other things like Jesus

> holding the huge crowd spellbound . . . "finding" the bread and fish to feed them . . . calming with His word the crashing waves . . . preaching His disturbing message and debating His detractors . . . standing there as His followers silently left Him (John 6:42, 52, 60, 66).

After Jesus calmed the storm the disciples were amazed, beyond measure, and "marveled" (Mark 6:51). Matthew says they "worshiped." That act of worship explains Peter's answer the next day to the question of Jesus, "Are you also going away?" Peter answered for all of them when he said, "Lord, to whom shall we go? You have the words of eternal life. Also, we have come to believe and know that You are the Christ, the Son of the Living God" (John 6:67–69).

At this moment I feel an enormous affection for Peter. Whatever remains of the self-centered, vainglorious, obtuse Galilean (and much does remain), he shows the effects of Jesus' nurturing ministry. Peter and his fellow disciples have just said something they could never have said a year before, maybe a week before—a sure sign that they have begun to grow, to change, to become "becomers."

That's what the last two days were all about. We conclude therefore that Jesus allowed these humanly disastrous events so His men could come to know Him and become like Him. Only in this light do His actions make sense. He was leading His men to grow.

The Development of Soul

We are often tempted to assume that growth is a simple process. Just read the Bible, pray every day, and you'll grow, grow, grow! We're convinced that the Word of God and the Holy Spirit are the only necessary agents for becoming spiritual. Forget the help of fellow believers! Forget the sanctifying effects of pain! It's just "Jesus and me on the Jericho Road."

But those who plunge deeply in the Christian walk know better. Chuck Colson, reviewing his twenty years as a Christian, confesses that his personal fulfillment came from prison, not from political or earthly power. He agrees with Solzhenitsyn that the meaning of earthly existence lies not, as we have grown used to thinking, in prosperity, but in the "development of soul."

That phrase, "development of soul," intrigues me. Jesus was committed to forging great-souled followers. The project required His disciples to undergo a full range of disciplines in the company of fellow strugglers, under the authority of His Word, and with His confirming presence. Jesus' concerns went way beyond skills or programs or methods or even ministry excellence. He was growing people who would know Him and know themselves and would thus be able to know and nurture others. Skills, methods, and programs would come in due season. And if we listen we may hear Peter, as an aged apostle, echo this same truth, "May the God of all grace, who called us into His eternal glory by Christ Jesus, *after you have suffered a while,* make you perfect, stablish, strengthen, settle you" (1 Peter 5:10).

Early in our ministry my wife, Esther, and I were going through a time of deep hurt. While visiting our hometown, I poured out my heart to Pastor John. I complained, with some bitterness, that God seemed to be my enemy instead of my friend. There were moments when I felt an urgent need for Him, and He didn't seem to be there. John proved to be a true mentor. He heard me out with never a flinch or rebuke and extended his acceptance, care, concern, and wise counsel. Under his guidance and the grace of God, a bit more "soul" took shape in the heart of a discouraged young pastor.

The soul grows and matures through both pain and pleasure under the watchful eyes of God and faithful human mentors who know how to stand by in times of both trouble and success. To grow leaders, the kneading process must develop the soul.

Reflection/Discussion
1. Discuss with another what might be implied in growing "from the inside out" (see Gal. 5:22–23).
2. Why is a love relationship so important for growth?
3. How is God using pain to nurture you toward growth?

Endnotes
1. Sherman and Hendricks, *Your Work Matters to God*, 245.

The disciples, so very human, knew the pain of ruptured relationships. They saw it and felt it. In the third training stage, Jesus draws on their experience to lead them into a painful learning process. His goal is to enlarge their relational capacity, increase their sensitivity to others, and strengthen their capacity to lead. This portion of the story is uniquely pointed and practical. When reading this chapter, notice:

- the priority of relationships,

- the broad range of human pain,

- the dullness of the disciples,

- that leading requires relating.

• 5 •

Teaching Them to Relate

There is a deep hunger in the human soul for relationships with significant other persons. When asked about the connection between physical health and loneliness, a prominent university professor replied that "companionship is as important to our health as the air we breathe. In fact, companionship is often taken for granted . . . until we are deprived of it. The fact is that social isolation, the sudden loss of love, and chronic loneliness, are significant contributors to death."[1]

In the company of Jesus, the disciples learned some deep and practical lessons about the importance of relationships—with each other and with those outside the group. The learning took place against the background of significant events:

- Caesarea Phillippi, scene of the pivotal moment when Peter confessed the deity of Jesus (Mark 8:27);
- the Transfiguration, when three disciples shared a breathtaking view of His kingdom (Mark 9:1);
- a valley experience, as Jesus began to announce His upcoming death—a theme that was ever after at the surface of His thoughts (Mark 8:31; 9:30; 10:33).

Immediately following, we are introduced to the next stage of development—learning about relationships.

57

A Relational Disturbance

The tone is set in Mark 10:35–45. When the other ten disciples heard of the favor requested by James and John, they were angry. J. B. Phillips sees them as "highly indignant." In response to this relational conflict, Jesus delivered a short but potent sermon. It speaks to the issue of leadership, but it was triggered by a crisis in relationships. With this background, we can read the rest of the story.

"But calling them to Himself, Jesus said to them, 'You know that those who are considered rulers over the Gentiles lord it over them, and their great ones exercise authority over them. Yet it shall not be so among you; but whoever desires to become great among you shall be your servant. And whoever of you desires to be first shall be slave of all. For even the Son of Man did not come to be served, but to serve, and to give His life a ransom for many'" (Mark 10:42–45).

This isn't the first time the issue of relationships has been raised. The Sermon on the Mount is filled with it. But that famous sermon, though spoken in the presence of the disciples, was aimed chiefly at the crowd (Matt. 7:28–29). Furthermore, the mastery of relationships requires more than a sermon. It calls for personal interactions around life-related experiences. This is the unique contribution of Mark's story, and his emphasis comes at just the right time.

Mark 9:30 to 10:52 deserves careful reading. Note its mood and tone. In the glow of this central crisis (10:35–45), a series of events come alive, highlighting the need for the disciples to master the art of relationships. Using these real-life experiences, Jesus draws out a series of life-transforming lessons.

Lessons in Relationships

"What were you talking about along the way?" He asked (9:33–37). They admitted, with embarrassment, to discussing who was the greatest. Anticipating the point He would stress later, Jesus said that anyone who wants to be chief must become a servant (9:35).

Lesson: *Self-centered comparisons bring competition.*

Taking up a little child in His arms, Jesus said, "Whoever receives one of these little children in my name receives me" (9:38–41). But almost before the words left His lips, John blurted out, "Master, we saw one casting out demons in your name and he did not follow us, and we forbade him." With a stern rebuke for intolerance, Jesus called for a generous spirit toward all who follow Him, even those from other groups.

Lesson: *Discernment, yes! Judgmentalism, no!*

Here Jesus implied that anyone who offended the "weak" (little ones), could end up with a millstone around his neck (9:42). One who demeaned fellow human beings was guilty of a terrible sin, and Jesus made it clear that such behavior is unacceptable in circles where He is Lord.

Lesson: *Don't brutalize people.*

As the crowd milled about, parents thronged the Lord, imploring Him to bless their babies (10:13–16). As He reached for the infants, the disciples "rebuked" them. In one of the most winsome episodes in the New Testament, Jesus indignantly responded, "Let the children come to me . . . do not forbid them."

Lesson: *Reach out—don't turn people off!*

After the conversation with the rich ruler, Peter reminded Jesus that he and the others had indeed left everything to follow Him (10:28–31). "What do we get in return?" he asked. Jesus answered that His followers will receive a hundred times more "brothers, sisters, mothers, and children," a reference, no doubt, to the rich relationships of the kingdom of God.

Lesson: *None are richer in relationships than members of the family of God.*

In 10:35–45 we return to the central text, this time to note its leadership implications. The truth comes through clearly. He who would lead must serve. Then comes the great pronouncement, the secret of His own ministry, "For even the Son of Man came not to be ministered unto but to minister, and to give His life a ransom for many."

Lesson: *To be leaders, we must be servants.*

As Jesus and His group entered Jericho, a blind beggar cried vainly by the wayside (10:46–52). People tried to hush him up, but he only shouted the louder. Jesus, hearing him, "stood still." As the crowd milled and moved, confused and self-absorbed, the

Son of God listened to the cry of a blind old beggar. More than that, He called the beggar to His side and healed him.

Lesson: *Master the "awesome power of the listening heart."* [2]

The disciples learned that becoming a relating person is neither quick nor easy. Each of the episodes involved a level of emotional distress, illustrating that relational competence is often gained through rupture followed by healing. Instead of quiet little classrooms and academic lectures, Jesus and His men shared a mobile laboratory where they felt the thrust and counterthrust of conflict, intrusive questions, sobering answers, and persistent probing of thoughts and emotions.

Growing in Relationships

These lessons deserve a review. Self-centeredness, rejection, offense, callousness, relational isolation, arrogance, and an inability to hear people in pain destroy relationships. But relationships are strengthened as we esteem those around us, accept them, look out for their welfare, care for them, remain in touch, serve them, and listen.

Fit the pieces together and they spell *love*. Mark doesn't use the word in this section, but it appears in 12:28–31 when Jesus refers to the first commandment, namely, to "love God." The second requires that we love our neighbor as ourselves.

"Does this stuff really matter? Aren't relationships just fluff and feathers?" someone asks. Don Baker tells of a young Christian who was attending four churches at the same time. She was looking for a church "where the Scriptures are taught so I can understand them, and the truth made portable so I can live it." But she wanted more.

"I want a church," she said, "where (people) love each other as much as they profess to love Christ, . . . where relationships go deeper than the masks we wear, . . . I'm really looking for . . . meaningful relationships. I (hoped) to find them in church, and I'm disappointed that I haven't."

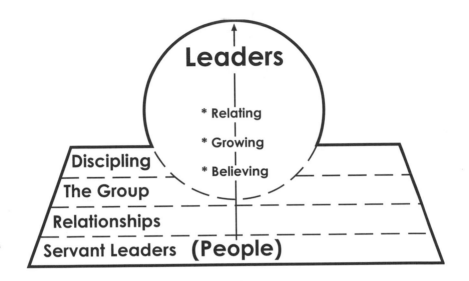

Figure 7

Listen to that plaintive appeal, and the truth will hit you in the face: the tragedy in today's church is relational poverty! Our poverty will give ground only as more of us are believing, growing toward maturity, and experiencing freedom from competition, rejection, brutality, rudeness, selfishness, insensitivity, and unconcern.

Conclusion

But is change really possible? Can any of us, regardless of habits or temperament, grow toward quality biblical relationships?

Ron Klassen, director of Rural Home Missionary Association, a small-town church planting ministry, tells his own story of how a type A person learned to show concern for people. Like many of us, Ron was task-driven. As a young preacher, he figured that his church would be transformed if he spent his time preparing solid Bible messages. But after his sermons and good management failed to make the expected impact, he concluded that he needed to become a more balanced leader in order to minister to the whole body of Christ, not just other type A people.[3]

The project was tough. He didn't want to be a phony, but deep down he knew he cared about people. He just didn't know how to show it. So he began building "people concerns" into his life at critical points—prayer times, "to do" lists, appointment calendar, even his preaching. Yes, even his preaching changed! Still thoroughly biblical, he was now speaking God's truth to real human needs.

Ron is still a type A person because that's how God made him. But by God's grace and Ron's diligent commitment, he is able to express type B concerns. In his own words, he has "grown to seek out people more and enjoy people." He further adds, "It used to take sheer discipline for me to set aside tasks for people, but now I enjoy people and look forward to people experiences. This would not have happened had I not forced myself to manifest 'Type B' characteristics when I would rather have run from people."

Judge for yourself! Was the change difficult? Sure! Was it possible? Of course! And it made a world of ministry difference.

Reflection/Discussion
1. Read Mark 10:35–45 in two versions. With another person, discuss the background of this conflict among the disciples.
2. Can you think of examples where relationships have been hurt by self-centered comparisons, rejection, offense, callousness, relational isolation, arrogance, inability to hear?
3. How can the negatives be turned into positives?

Endnotes
1. Don Baker, *Restoring Broken Relationships* (Eugene, OR: Harvest House, 1989).

2. John W. Drakeford, *The Awesome Power of the Listening Heart* (Grand Rapids: Zondervan, 1982).

3. Ron Klassen, "Can Type As Care About People?" *Leadership* (1994).

The passion and death of Jesus Christ is an event of such enormous import for Jesus and for us that we can easily ignore its unique effect on the disciples. But living through the passion week, with all its anguish, was part of the process of their development. In this stage Jesus focuses on the need for "vision." For these men to be effective leaders, they must learn to "aspire." When reading this chapter, notice:

- the role of the mentor,

- that aspiring grows out of relating,

- that learning to aspire is a process,

- that vision is reflected in action,

- the effects of a completed leadership development program on the disciples.

• 6 •

Stimulating Them to Aspire

What is *vision?* Surely something more than being a mystical "visionary," which is often little more than looking into a foggy future. It has been wisely said that great ideas need landing gear as well as wings! At the most basic level, *vision is a conviction that, by God's grace, I can make a difference in the kingdom of God.* It's more than an ability to clearly see a future reality—it's a *capacity* for vision that predates and outlasts any one task, a deep inner sense that I can be of value to the cause of Christ.

Vision Is Catching

During their final stage of training, the disciples caught this sense of vision. When they stood, finally, on the other side of the Cross, they were aspiring men. In Mark 11–16 we learn how Jesus transferred the gift of vision and how we can share it with others today.

He modeled it as He began living out the last days of His earthly life. It started with His entry into Jerusalem (11:1–11). The disciples watched as Jesus cursed the fig tree, entered the city, cleansed the temple, and debated enemies (chapters 11 and 12). In all this, Mark portrays a person of vision. The first step in sharing vision is an ability to model it. *Vision is born as people rub shoulders with those who have it.*

He shared His view of the future in the Olivet discourse (chapter 13). As the disciples listened, Jesus told them of glorious events yet to come, climaxing with the inauguration of His coming kingdom (13:26). There is no better way to create vision than to take followers into our confidence. *Vision in transmitted as followers share the pulse of the leader's passion.*

He permitted His men to fail for the Shepherd was smitten and the sheep scattered. In all of Mark's record there is not one reference to the disciples during the actual crucifixion. In lonely gardens and shrouded homes they were hiding. This, too, was part of the process. In the lives of those God uses, there may be great failure. Leaders in the making often find that *vision grows in the valleys of life.*

He mediated forgiveness and reconciliation when He met His men after the Resurrection. Jesus' pledge to regather them in Galilee is of great significance (14:27). Both Matthew and Mark tell of the angel who commanded the women to announce the postresurrection meeting. Put the pieces all together and you have a magnificent story of Jesus restoring the broken band of disciples. As five of them were fishing, they met Jesus (John 21). He restored Peter, with the others, then all together on a mountain in Galilee, perhaps the one where they were first appointed. *Vision is nourished in a healing community.*

He defined their task . . . when He commissioned them. Preach the Gospel to every creature, make disciples, witness—here at home, in Samaria, around the world, and I will never leave you. *Vision grows in the face of an exciting venture.*

He pointed them toward Pentecost as He prepared to return to the Father. He told His disciples of the Holy Spirit, and that the Holy Spirit would come to indwell them (see Mark 16:19 with Luke 24:49–53 and John 14:16–18). To prepare for this event they were commanded to wait in Jerusalem. It happened as Jesus said (Acts 2:22–47). *Vision is the fruit of the Holy Spirit in our lives.*

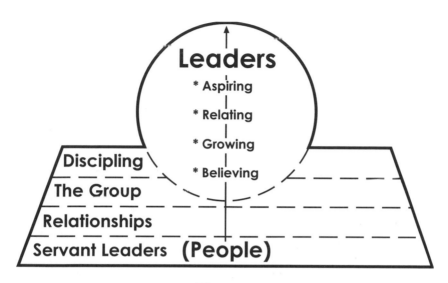

Figure 8

Men Who Aspired

The Evidence

The vision of the disciples expressed itself even prior to Pentecost, when they took steps to keep their number at full strength (Acts 1:15–26). Whether or not we agree with their action or their selection, their gaze was toward the future (Acts 1:12–14). I also find it instructive that Justus and Matthias were considered part of the company Jesus trained. Peter reminds his friends that the one chosen to replace Judas must have been a beneficiary of Jesus' training ministry—having "accompanied us all the time that the Lord Jesus went in and out among us, beginning from the baptism of John to the day when He was taken up from us." To serve as a witness to the Resurrection, the person must meet the criteria.

Jesus trained more than twelve disciples, more than seventy, maybe more than one hundred and twenty. The Twelve were distinguished more by their apostolic appointment than by the uniqueness of their preparation. Justus and Matthias, along with others, were up to speed.

A Completed Phase

So here they are, twelve disciples—believing, growing, relating, and aspiring—ready to lead and be followed. Mark says they went out and "preached the Word everywhere, the Lord working with them and confirming the Word through accompanying signs. Amen" (16:20)! [1]

Because of questions concerning manuscript genuineness, Mark 6:9–20 is not usually used to define the person and ministry of the Spirit. But genuine or not, the time frame, which parallels the other three gospels, takes us to and beyond the Pentecost event. Furthermore, Matthew, Luke, and John bear witness that the disciples were ready to fulfill their commission (Matt. 28:18–20; Luke 24:46–48, John 21:15–25). Hebrews 2:3–4 is also important. We read that after the proclamation of the Gospel by Jesus Himself, it was "confirmed to us by those who heard Him, God also bearing witness both with signs and wonders." Whomever else this means, it surely includes the Twelve.

Extrabiblical sources also support the conclusion that the apostles, upon the completion of their training, went forth to preach the Gospel and to lead the people of God; historians are treating these apostolic traditions much more seriously than previously.[2]

An Incomplete Process

A phase of training was completed, but the process continued, for Jesus never stops striving to turn His people into "becomers" (Phil. 1:6). When we claim, therefore, that the disciples were believing, growing, relating, and aspiring, we aren't saying they were finished products. Remember, the words are believ*ing*, grow*ing*, relat*ing*, and aspir*ing*. Until we see Christ face-to-face, the process must go on. We ought never stop believing, growing, relating, and aspiring. The disciples completed a phase, but the process continued.

They had much ground to cover and many major battles to fight. Still ahead were many gritty issues, like getting the new church off the ground, full obedience to the commands of their Lord, Peter's visit to the house of Cornelius, Gentile salvation, the Jerusalem Council, conflict between Peter and Paul, conflict between Paul and Barnabas over Mark—and ever so much more.

They would confront the possibility of fear and failure and

defeat as long as they lived. But through it all, they would keep on believing, growing, relating, and aspiring until they died. That's why Jesus announced, before His departure, an in-service training program under the supervision of the Holy Spirit, with no terminal point short of death or His return (John 16:12–15). These men understood the program and gladly acknowledged their human imperfections. They would have agreed that it is expecting too little not to expect change in your behavior as you grow in Christ but that it is "expecting too much to think that change will come without a struggle."[3]

The process was not finished, but they were changing! Peter was a different man at Pentecost than before. Though he was not yet the man he would be, he was on the way—like the others. They were men of faith, marked by growth, alive to relationships, and *gripped by vision*—moving toward their potentials under the grace of God—*qualified leaders in the kingdom of God*

Conclusion

Is it happening today? Yes, but few are aware of it. The prevailing Christian mood does not allocate much attention to an event that is not easily quantifiable.

In the late 1960s, when the discipling theme became prominent, I grieved over my disadvantaged state. No one had ever discipled me. But as I reviewed the New Testament, especially the ministry of Jesus, the burden lifted. I had indeed been discipled, but the process was so normal that the one being mentored, at least, was not acutely conscious of it. Yet the components were there—the healthy group, authentic relationships, servant leaders, and mentoring!

In that climate, Pastor John did his work. He accepted me, believed in me, took seriously my early convictions for ministry, gave me a chance to serve, and encouraged me. Though I was in my early twenties and he in his late thirties, we shared often about the challenge of Christian living, theology, books, preaching, and how the church functions. He allowed me to watch as the crises came along, with no attempt to clone me in his image. He and his wife opened their home, treated us as family, fed us, joked with us, and prayed with us. I do not stretch the truth when I say that, under God, Pastor John gave me my ministry. And in giving me a ministry, he gave me vision.

Reflection/Discussion

1. Discuss with another how vision is caught by:

    *   rubbing shoulders with those who have it,
    *   sharing the hopes and dreams of leaders,
    *   having honest mentors who allow failure,
    *   a healing, forgiving community,
    *   a clearly defined and challenging task,
    *   the work of the Holy Spirit.

2. Read Acts 20:17–38 and 1 Peter 5:1–7 and examine the ways Paul and Peter encouraged vision.
3. How can you increase your vision?

End Notes

1. Vincent Taylor, *The Gospel According to Mark* (New York: Macmillan, 1959), quotes Sir A. F. Hort, 28–51; Henry Barclay Swete, ciii–cxiii; and Albert Lagrange, 456–68.

2. McBirnie, *The Search for the Twelve Apostles.*

3. Mike Bellah, *Baby Boom Believers* (Wheaton IL: Tyndale House, 1988).

Section Three
The Pattern Confirmed

Two thousand years stand between us and the life of Jesus of Nazareth. Can we be sure that what He preached and practiced applies to us today? More importantly, does it work? These are the questions we answer in section 3.

Chapter 7 speaks to the witness of the early church. Did the first century church follow Jesus' pattern Do we know for sure? How do we know? When reading this chapter, notice:

- that the pattern of Peter, Paul, James, and John resembles that of Jesus,

- that each element of Jesus' pattern is reflected in the early church,

- that "believing, growing, relating, and aspiring" are clearly featured,

- the example of John Mark.

• 7 •

The First-Century Witness

Effective Christian leaders are marked by *faith, growth, relationships*, and *vision*—four key empowering words derived from Mark's gospel. They're *believing, growing, relating, and aspiring persons*. Where these qualities are found, you find leaders. And where biblical leaders are found, these qualities are found.

At the end of the last chapter we saw how important these words are. They must be taken seriously.

1. They arise directly from the flow of Mark's gospel.
2. Servant leaders can transmit these qualities to others, so they must not be confused with temperament traits, talents, or learned skills.
3. They express a "state of being" required of those who aspire to be Christian leaders.
4. They offer an effective way of measuring progress.
5. They reflect a dynamic process because the qualities can be reproduced in one phase (a sequence of stages), yet more deeply reproduced as recurring phases produce a continuous process.

That's the pattern! Jesus made it work once. But did it work in the early church? And can it work today?

A generation ago Robert Coleman authored a pacesetting

73

book, *The Master Plan of Evangelism,* committed to the proposition that the world can only be reached by the process of multiplication, not addition.[1] Discipling, of course, is the multiplication method.

More recently he wrote a follow-up book, *The Master Plan of Discipleship*, to find out whether the early church followed Jesus' pattern. Did they honor His Word?[2] Coleman's evidence is impressive and his conclusion inescapable. In both outreach and leadership ministry, the church did what Jesus taught them to do. Whether we think of it as

- servant leadership
- relational leadership
- transforming leadership
- integrative leadership

the early Christians understood it and honored it.

The Church at Large

Time and again in the Acts and Epistles the basic features of Jesus' training ministry are worked out.

Servant Leaders

John, writing to Gaius, commends him for faithfully serving the brethren and strangers, all of whom bore witness of his "love" to the church. He then rebukes the arrogant Diotrephes and applauds the gracious Demetrius (3 John).

Peter urges church elders to "feed (pasture) the flock of God." They are not to be "lords over" God's heritage, but "examples" to the flock (1 Peter 5).

James warns teachers of their responsibility to be pure, peaceable, gentle, and approachable; full of mercy and good fruits, and without partiality and hypocrisy (James 3:1–17).

Paul reminds the Ephesian elders that he had lived "among" them, serving the Lord with all humility, tears, and temptations and had taught them publicly and privately (house to house). He exhorts them to "feed" (pasture) the flock, to love it and guard it (Acts 20:17–38).

Relationships

The theme of relationships pervades the New Testament

from beginning to end. Especially in the Epistles, one passage after the other sparkles with interest. Romans 12 is a good place to begin. Here Paul sees the church as a "body" with many "members," each having different "gifts" and diverse ministries. He reminds us that believers, in a properly working body, will show mercy, love without sham, and be kind and affectionate. They will honor fellow Christians and freely dispense material help to those in need. When Christians rejoice, friends rejoice with them. When they weep, their friends grieve. Rather than seek revenge, they allow God to judge, and as much as possible they live at peace with everyone, doing good even to their enemies.

But this is just a start. As Gene Getz reminds us, the Epistles bear witness to the need for believers to dynamically relate to "one another."[3] Robert Coleman puts it beautifully when he says that just as Jesus lived with His disciples, so God's people "formed an on-going communion" of the Spirit. It was in this Spirit-empowered community that the relationship between leader and follower "provided the environment for their training." Church leaders "sensed a priority to spend time with persons training for leadership."[4]

A French writer studied the lives of the monarchs of France. He found only three who were reared by their natural mothers, the rest were cared for by relatives or hired nurses. He was stunned to discover that, of the total, only three were known to have loved the French people. Guess which three?

Just as children experiencing the natural love of their parents learn to love others, leaders maturing in a climate of acceptance, love, and godly discipline grow to accept, love, serve, disciple, and lead others.

The Group

Early church leaders, following Jesus' example, cared about community. They surrounded themselves with groups of people who served as they were being trained. Peter's group included the twelve apostles, Silvanus, Mark, and perhaps others. John, the Beloved Apostle, also had his "brethren," some of whom were cast out of the church by the proud Diotrephes (3 John). And Paul had his group. Aside from Timothy, Titus, and Luke, Aristarchus, Secundus, Gaius, Sopater, Tychicus, and Trophimus can be listed (Acts 20:4). Mark and Demas are named in

2 Timothy, Epaphras in Colossians, and Epaphroditus in Philippians.

Some were with Paul almost continually. We can speak as easily of "Paul and his men" as of "Jesus and His men." Paul, too, allowed his men to learn by doing. Timothy was sent to Ephesus, Titus to Crete. Tychicus was dispatched to Ephesus to replace Timothy, because Timothy was needed by Paul in Rome.

The pattern of Paul was so familiar that Timothy needed only a passing reminder. "The things that you have heard from me among many witnesses, the same commit to faithful men who shall be able to teach others also" (2 Tim. 2:2). Jesus, Paul, and the others knew that the leadership ideal is neither a lone ranger nor a leaderless group, but a leader among fellow leaders.

Discipling

Coleman reminds us that in Matthew 28:19, the Greek words for "go," "baptizing," and "teaching" are participles. The commands "derive their direction from the leading verb, 'make disciples'" i.e., "As you go, make disciples."

In giving discipling such a high priority, Jesus was commanding His followers to "do what He had done." He was defining His ministry method. Though it was slow and required sacrifice, He "knew His way would succeed." [5]

Long before imitative learning was rediscovered by Albert Bandura, it was practiced by Jesus. *Discipling* was the word Jesus used. Another good word is *mentoring*.

Ron Lee Davis sees mentoring as a process of living for the next generation. In his book on this theme, *Mentoring: Strategy of the Master*, Davis refers to the king in Homer's *Odyssey* who goes to war and entrusts his son to the care of his friend, "Mentor." Mentor thus becomes the model of a wise and caring counselor who, by the genuineness of his life, earns respect and trust. With this model in mind, Davis writes about his first church, in rural Iowa, with about eighty members, where he met a thirty-five-year-old fellow named Dean Frost. Frost was married and had a great wife and two teenage daughters. Davis was seminary trained, Frost was not. Davis was a professional man, Frost worked with his hands.

Frost was only a few years older than Davis, yet the impact of Frost on the life and ministry of Davis was incalculable. This rural plumber was just one in a long line of mentors in the life of Ron Lee Davis. Their cumulative impact led him to say that though he highly values his academic training, when he looks back over all the influences that have shaped his mind, values, faith, and character, he has to conclude that his life has been impacted far more dramatically by a few important people, his mentors, than by the formal educational process. Sounds like the New Testament, doesn't it?

To quote Coleman again, "The church did not erect colleges or theological seminaries! To mold the life of the members, they simply got learners and teachers together in natural settings where they lived and worked every day. Nothing was new. . . . The church . . . was following the same approach . . . their Lord had used." [6]

Colleges and seminaries are valuable and not to be despised. But if institutionalized learning is not undergirded by a kneading process, the resulting leadership will be mediocre at best, and maybe even harmful.

The Example of Paul

Paul's fidelity to Jesus' example is especially noteworthy, coming through clearly in 2 Timothy. Oswald Sanders suggests that the letter was written at a time when Timothy was floundering and needing help.[7] The book may thus be a reaffirmation of the principles Paul used in Timothy's original training. If so, it appears that Paul was concerned with the same four transferable qualities Jesus dealt with. The parallels are uncanny.

Paul's first concern is Timothy's *faith*, which he says is "unfeigned" (1:3–5). Timothy is a believing man, and Paul sees his faith as the foundation of his life and ministry. Timothy must keep his faith strong.

Paul urges Timothy to *grow*, to "stir up the gift" (1:6). Timothy has the potential of power, love, and self-control (1:7), and hence must not be ashamed of Jesus or of Paul (1:8). He is to hold fast Paul's words (1:13) and "be strong" (2:1). After this exhortation, Paul coins a series of metaphors (son, soldier, athlete, farmer, workman, vessel, servant) to pinpoint Timothy's growth goals (2 Tim. 2).

In 2 Timothy 2:14–26 the theme of *relationships* is stressed. In the midst of pressing duties, Timothy may have allowed his relationships to atrophy. Paul prods him to refurbish them. "Remind them . . . not to strive" (2:14). "Shun useless babblings"

(2:16). "Pursue righteousness, love, peace" (2:22). "Avoid foolish questions" (2:23). "A servant . . . must not quarrel" (2:24). He should be "gentle and patient" (2:24). And "in meekness" he should instruct "those who oppose themselves" (2:25).

Finally, like Jesus in the Olivet Discourse, Paul renews Timothy's _vision_. He reminds him that things will get worse instead of better (3:1–13). But since Timothy has been well trained, he is a qualified "man of God" (3:14–17) and can face the task that looms ahead (4:1–5). Then, again like Jesus, he says "I am about to leave. Get on with your task. The Lord will be with you" (4:6–22).

Believing, growing, relating, aspiring! These are the concerns that breathe new vigor into the discouraged disciple. They were probably the centerpiece of Paul's concern as he trained his young helper in the first place.

The Saga of John Mark

Mark's life spans the New Testament from the Crucifixion to the destruction of Rome. If our guess is correct, Mark was the youth who ran naked from Gethsemane after escaping the clutches of an arresting soldier. He reappears at strategic points throughout the next three decades, with a final appearance in Paul's second letter to Timothy, and just before Paul's martyrdom. Mark's experience is therefore an appropriate window through which to catch another view of how the teaching and example of Jesus was worked out by His followers.

Reading the story only through Acts 15, which recounts his indefensible flight from Paul and Barnabas, we can assess Mark as nothing other than a first-rate failure (Acts 13:13; 15:36–41). But three decades later Paul refers to him in Colossians and Philemon as a "fellow worker." And as Paul suffered his final imprisonment, he asked Timothy to come and to bring John Mark, who is "profitable . . . for the ministry" (2 Tim. 4:11). Finally, of course, Mark had the honor of writing the second gospel.

As I study the career of this man from beginning to end, I find only one way to account for his amazing metamorphosis. Mark was transformed from failure to success because, by God's grace and providence, some people created a climate in which he could repent, reassess things, mature, learn, and be rehabilitated. And we need not look far to identify these people.

One, surprisingly, was Paul. Someone has said that a self-centered failure needs two kinds of helpers, one to knock him off his pedestal and the other to fish him out of the pond, dry him off, pat him on the back, and help him on his way. Paul admirably served the first purpose. Much as Mark surely resented Paul's criticism, it was true and he had to face it. Paul's break with Barnabas temporarily ruffled the climate of Mark's world, but he would learn later that Paul could forgive with the best of them.

Barnabas was the key. This man gave up all hope of ministry with Paul to strengthen his wobbly young nephew. The scene has power to moisten the eye—the great multicultural genius giving his remaining time and strength to rehabilitate a young failure.

Mark may have had a third helpful friend. We must ask whether Mark's recovery could have happened without Peter? While Peter's whereabouts are uncertain after Acts 12, it seems likely, given his leadership status, his relationship with Mark and his own failures, that the two met during these crucial days. Can't you hear the old warrior call his errant disciple to account, push him to make amends, to start over?

Whatever we decide about Peter's involvement, the elements of Jesus' leadership development ministry are all there:

- servant leaders
- relationships
- the group
- mentoring

As a crestfallen Mark began gathering himself together, he learned that being the leader God intended would require a major restructuring of his life. Fading faith, distorted growth, truncated relationships, and faulty vision had done him in. He needed a revitalized faith, renewed growth, restored relationships, and a refocused vision. His only hope was to become a believing, growing, relating, and aspiring man of God, and that's what God made him.

Conclusion

The early Christians did not work in the dark. They had a clear notion about how to lead, how to follow, and how to turn people into leaders. At no point does the New Testament offer aid and comfort to those who would adopt a rigid corporate model. At least ten major New Testament passages make strong statements about the nature of Christian leadership, and neither singly nor in concert do they encourage an authoritarian pattern. The passages I refer to are

- Mark 10, and its focus on servant leadership
- Acts 6, the apostles and first deacons
- Acts 15, the Jerusalem Council
- Acts 20, Paul's departure from the Ephesian elders
- 2 Corinthians 3–5, the obligations of the ministry
- Ephesians 4, the work of gifted men
- 1 Thessalonians 2, Paul's leadership in Thessalonica
- James 3, the counsel to teachers
- 1 Peter 5, the exhortation to elders
- 1 Timothy 2 and Titus 1, qualifications for church leaders

When we leave the teaching passages to examine the primary words used by New Testament writers, the findings are the same. Whether it's

- *hodegeo* (to lead the way)
- *exago* (to lead out)
- *kubernesis* (the helmsman of a ship)

all suggest the one who goes before, shows the way, serves as a model, and gives direction.

The idea of a distant, oppressive, controlling authority is not to be found. Even the command in Hebrews 13:17 to "obey" those who rule over us must not be interpreted as compliance to dictatorial leaders. If we would honor just this one principle, the unbiblical shepherding movements of the day would vanish.

Small-church pastors should be encouraged. As I said at the outset, the pattern is universally applicable. But in smaller churches, the interpersonal dynamics between pastor and people make it so imminently usable that flirtations with alternate options should be a minor temptation.

Remember that Pastor John, though founding a church that grew to significant size, defined his ministry in a congregation of less than one hundred. The word to my friends in smaller churches, then, is *go for it!*

Reflection/Discussion

1. Read the ten passages listed on page 80 and look for parallels between the pattern of Jesus and New Testament church leaders.

Endnotes

1. Robert E. Coleman, *The Master Plan of Evangelism* (Tarrytown, NY: Fleming H. Revell, 1964).

2. ———, *The Master Plan of Discipleship* (Tarrytown, NY: Fleming H. Revell, 1987).

3. Gene Getz, *The Measure of a Man* (Glendale, CA: G/L Publications, 1974).

4. Ibid.

5. Ibid.

6. Ibid.

7. Oswald J. Sanders, *Paul, the Leader* (Eastbourne, E. Sussex: Kingsway Publications, 1983), 167–68.

What has two thousand years of history done to Jesus' leadership pattern? Is it viable for today? Does God still expect His people to follow it? Does it still work? How do we know? Is there any evidence to go on? These questions with their answers connect Jesus' first century ministry to the challenges of today. The answer: Jesus' pattern is as viable today as two thousand years ago and remains in force for the church. When reading this chapter, notice:

- the essence of servant leadership,

- how the terms used by many of today's managers fit the biblical model,

- why "echoes" from the workplace ought to be listened to,

- how the ministries of Pastor John and Pastor Nussbaum interrelate. Compare the review of Pastor John's ministry in the introduction with the material in chapter 8.

• 8 •

The Contemporary Witness

The early church followed Jesus' pattern and it worked. But what evidence do we have that the centuries-old pattern is usable today? What contemporary witnesses can be called up? And what do they have to say?

Echoes from the Workplace

It may appear that we're starting with a strange echo—the American workplace—the people who gave us traditional management with its destructive characteristics. But during the past decade, a growing minority in corporate America has been rendering its own report on the question of leadership, and it's worth hearing.

Participative Management

The business changes over the past decade are so well known as to need little comment. Many are also aware that participative management has been largely responsible for these changes. Its tenets are not new. But ten years ago, in response to economic pressures, some tested ideas coalesced to form the "Participative Management" option. What may be less well known is the level of agreement, at practical points, between the "new management" and the biblical leadership model.

No one is suggesting that we should baptize participative management as Christian. But it's difficult to read comments from management authors about such things as values, the need to respect people, the benefit of team leadership, and the power of coaching and modeling, without seeing some connections between what they're saying and what we've been talking about.

Economic pressures have forced businesses to focus on team building and value sharing as never before. Teamwork, not adversarial relationships, increases production. Training supervisors to be counselors and coaches results in a more challenging workplace, a more rewarding job situation, and a more competitive company.

The Principles of Participative Management

The key ideas are coaching, collaboration, team building, peer influence, value sharing, and vision, designed to encourage quality, effectiveness, and excellence. It isn't surprising that some see a connection between these themes and the Judeo-Christian ethic. ServiceMaster is an excellent example. Its devotion to service springs from a corporate culture based on the beliefs of its founders, three devout Christians who started the company in 1947.

Geoffrey Lantos, a marketing professor, turns for his example to the book of Leviticus, to the Golden Rule, You shall love your neighbor as yourself. He says that the highest values of any society are found in the quality and integrity of the relationships among its people.

The Trailblazers

It would be easy to list several dozen companies, large and small, who have moved toward the participative option. One of these is the Saturn company, makers of the car by the same name. When General Motors committed itself to the Saturn idea, it chose to form a new subsidiary. It did so because the GM bureaucracy was too inflexible to allow leaders to do what they knew had to be done to design, build, distribute, market, and service a car that could compete and win in today's climate.

I bring the Saturn plant into the picture because of the best-selling book *The Seven Habits of Highly Effective People*. It has been chosen by leaders at the Saturn plant as outlining the management approach of the future. Author Stephen Covey bucks the secular tide, for example, when he insists that change happens "from the inside out" (a Christian viewpoint) rather than from the "outside in" (a secular viewpoint).

Though Covey warns that his book isn't religious, he tells of times when he personally prayed and read the psalms. The life of Joseph in the Bible happens to be his favorite story. He even alludes to confession of sin. But the things to watch for are his comments about values, honesty, self-scrutiny, character, and discipline. Relationships also rank high on his list of priorities, as well as the need to respect people and to be able to work with them.[1]

Another pioneer in participative management is the Herman Miller Company of Zeeland, Michigan. Max DePree, retired CEO of Herman Miller, is the author, among other titles, of *Leadership Is an Art*. For ten years prior to 1987, Herman Miller ranked seventh in total profits to investors among Fortune 500 companies, boasting the most productive employees in the industry. One hundred dollars invested in 1975 grew to five thousand dollars by 1986.

Herman Miller is an innovative company. The employees are the owners. All regular employees who have worked there for at least a year own stock, and over fifty percent purchase additional shares. The company also introduced a "silver parachutes" program for all employees with over two years of service in case an unfriendly take-over lead to a termination of employment.

In his foreword to *Leadership Is an Art,* James O'Toole of the University of California writes that most books present leaders "as charismatic personalities, showmen, cheer leaders, con artists, visionaries, autocrats, and circus stunt men. They bark orders and run around doing everybody else's work for them. But Max's idea of leadership is different. He knows from experience that . . . leadership is 'liberating people to do what is required of them in the most effective and humane way possible.'"

What does DePree believe about leadership? Among other things he says that

- good leaders respect people,
- believing precedes doing,
- relationships matter more than structures,
- people are capable of growing.

The ground of his belief is that quality leaders must be committed to the value of the individual, to the belief that we are made in the image of God. And here we're in touch with the real thing, for Max DePree is a confessing Christian.

Cultural Factors

How do we account for these ideas and practices?

Many of us have already learned that Christian values are sometimes honored in circles that go way beyond the church. A Christian who attended a management seminar was impressed when a workshop leader challenged people to "respect others" and even called for them to "love people." The attendee expressed appreciation, suggesting that the comments resembled those of Jesus. Far from being flattered, the speaker was insulted, noting that he "hadn't been inside a church for years."

But whether admitted or not, the connection was real, and it can happen in more than one way.

The Bible tells us that human beings, though unregenerate, can intuitively know through general revelation about God, judgment, right, and wrong.

Those reared in Christian homes and communities, though not believers, may continue to be influenced by Christian values. Businesspeople, educators, sports personalities, journalists, or entertainers may reflect their Christian heritage.

We Christians also live in our culture; if we are committed to our faith, we too can make a difference.

It is painful but true: God sometimes speaks to His people through the culture around them, for the children of darkness can be wiser than the children of light. So God may be telling us through these echoes from the workplace that there is another way to lead. If secular leadership experts are sensing that something is wrong and needs fixing, the church should go back to the original leadership plan and get it right.

The Voice from the Church

When we move from the workplace to the church, we hear not an echo, but a voice. Although the voice of the church is not as strong as we'd like it to be, many pastors and churches make a serious effort to honor Jesus' pattern of leadership and get in touch with its essence.

This essence can't be reduced to a glitzy motto, but the phrases that keep drifting back are "respect for persons" and "love for people." At the heart of the Bible's pattern is a respect for persons so deep that it leads to a genuine love for people. If respect for persons is defined by the image of God in us and the value of Christ's death for us, we have a basis for relationships. The source of this relational thrust is *mature Christian personhood*, through which the truth can be lived out—by a believing, growing, relating, aspiring Christian.

Two Contemporary Examples

I have lived closely with two leaders who have reflected these qualities of mature Christian personhood and who have lived out the relationships. One was Pastor John. The other is Milo Nussbaum.

Milo Nussbaum, the founding pastor of Grace Evangelical Mennonite Church in Morton, Illinois, began the church thirty-five years ago with a congregation of about forty. In 1958 the population of Morton was five thousand. Grace Church is familiar to me because our family worshiped there from its inception until we moved away in 1966. During those years Milo was our pastor. We've remained friends and colleagues over the years, and since our ministry has now led us back to the area, we're again enjoying personal fellowship.

Healthy Transition

This congregation is a witness to biblical leadership because of the work of Pastor Nussbaum who, after leading his people for thirty-three years of healthy church life, stepped back from his senior pastoral position, allowed the church to call a successor, and permitted the man to lead. Today, Morton has a population of fifteen thousand and Grace Church, led by senior pastor Doug Habegger, has a congregation of eight hundred.

Pastor Habegger cites two factors that contributed to a healthy transition:

First, Pastor Nussbaum's longevity earned him the trust and confidence of the congregation so that when he retired, both leaders and congregation trusted his sense of timing. They knew that he made his decision unselfishly, in the best interests of the church.

Second, Pastor Nussbaum possessed the rare ability to trust younger and less-experienced men. This made it possible to entrust responsibilities into their care, knowing that the ministry was the Lord's and not his own.

At his retirement, the people sensed his confidence that the Lord would continue to build the church under new and younger pastoral guidance. He has been my cheerleader, and the congregation has followed his gracious example, which is a tribute to Pastor Nussbaum's mentoring ministry. He knew that for Grace to have a fruitful ministry after his retirement, it was crucial to develop younger leaders at the lay and professional levels. When he retired, a cross-generational team was in place. The transition is a tribute to Milo Nussbaum. I was a benefactor of that which God gave us through his leadership.[2]

The Fruit

Milo Nussbaum's leadership is seen in the fruitful ministry of Grace Church. It is Pastor Nussbaum's conviction that "the main things are the plain things and the plain things are the main things."

One of these main and plain things is *intercessory prayer*. From the beginning, specific prayer times were set aside, including at the opening of each board meeting. At the start of one meeting a board member gave Milo a resignation letter. But after a period of prayer, he asked for it back. He never did resign, he never quit serving, and two decades later was still a productive and joyful part of the church.

Relationships is another main and plain thing. The principle was tested when a new family moved to town and began attending the services. A well-meaning member informed Milo that the man was an "unruly brother" and should be watched. But Milo and others took time to love the man and his family and build relationships with them. It became clear that he had leadership potential, and in due course was given a new believers Sunday school class. He later assumed other significant leadership positions. Never once did he cause trouble. Milo says that strong relationships have life-changing effects, and that "what one is, is not the same as what one can be."

Another of Milo's main and plain things is the priority of *caring*. The church faced a crisis when a teenager and his brother were broad-sided by a car while they were riding a motorcycle. The older boy died the same day but the younger one lived for seven agonizing months. As the pain went on, Grace Church demonstrated what it means to "bear each other's burdens, and so fulfill the law of Christ." Pastor Nussbaum is convinced that "the work of the Spirit produces the fruit of the Spirit and when fruit becomes visible, everyone knows that the glorious body of Christ, the church, is at work."

Conclusion

Grace Church and the church founded by John Hiestand are each unique. They exist in different states, reflect different cultures, have had different experiences, and the members of the congregations have different temperaments and gifts. Their founding pastors never knew each other. Yet the men who led them had much in common.

1. Both were men of maturity, able to show respect and love for people. Flesh and blood men they were, but certainly believing, growing, relating, and aspiring men.
2. For both, relationships mattered, and they lived that conviction in daily life.
3. They were able to combine their relational competence with their organizing and managing work so that they strengthened their churches as they led their people.
4. Each of them ministered to one congregation over many years yet had grace to step back, allow a successor to be chosen, and let the successor lead.
5. Their churches developed leaders because the primary elements were there—servant leaders, relationships, group-building and community, and lots of mentoring.

How many pastors honor the pattern? Surely not enough. And those who do are usually quiet and unpretentious, write few books, and rarely go on lecture circuits. They are set apart, eventually, by their ministries which seem to glow, as the years pass by, with special luster. It is such pastors and churches that serve, today, as a primary witness to the undiminished practicality of biblical leadership.

Pastor Nussbaum founded a church that grew to substantial size, but his leadership ministry was defined in a congregation of less than one hundred. The pattern of Jesus is simple, like Pastor John's, and it is equally accessible. All that is required is for us to open our eyes, take it, and apply it.

Reflection/Discussion

1. Read a few current business periodicals and note any participative management themes that connect to ideas discussed in this book.
2. Read a newspaper or two for three weeks and take note of similar data.
3. Discuss with others the similarities and differences between Jesus' pattern and participative management.

Endnotes

1. Stephen Covey, *The Seven Habits of Highly Effective People* (New York: Simon and Schuster, 1989).

2. Doug Habegger, Written statement to Harold L. Longenecker, December, 1993.

Section Four

The Pattern at Work

Why are we concerned about growing when our theme is leadership? Aren't most Christian leaders growing? If one is regularly in the Word and busy with ministry, isn't growth a sure thing? Clearly, no! Just as priests in the Old Testament could live in the temple, yet despise God's name, profane His table, and lead people to stumble at the law (Mal. 1), church leaders today can know the Bible and be active in ministry, yet stop growing and hit the skids. When this happens, God's glory is dimmed and His work harmed. We can defend ourselves against this disaster only by maintaining a dynamic growth experience. When reading this section, notice:

- the nature of growth,

- the consequences of aborted growth,

- the beginning point for new growth,

- the story of "Sam,"

- that we lead well only as we grow.

• 9 •

Leading As We Grow

To shift allegiance from one deeply held view to another can be unnerving—not unlike gazing out a parked airplane window, noting with pleasure that you're finally moving, only to experience a momentary mental jolt when it turns out that it's the other guy who's moving, not you. That weird "thunk" announces a collision between the status quo and an unexpected new reality. Stephen Covey uses the term "paradigm shift" to explain this phenomenon. It's the shock of confronting a reality that "supersedes (our) present limited perception."[1]

If we ever grasp the difference between simply looking for leaders or growing them, between those who have merely mastered the techniques of the corporate model or servant leaders who are believing, growing, relating, and aspiring, we, too, may experience the shock of a new reality and feel a disconcerting thunk. In fact, my aim, in this final section, is to push us closer to that critical moment, that thunk of reality, by showing that

1. true servant leadership can happen only as a leader is believing, growing, relating, and aspiring—changing from the inside out;
2. healthy influence, the key to leadership, is the property of those who possess these leadership qualities;
3. how we lead determines how we do everything else.

Because the quality of growth has such huge implications, I begin here. Without faith, of course, there is no Christian leadership at all. But without growth, all other qualities are diminished, including faith. Without growth, faith is stagnant, relationships atrophy, and vision fogs up and dies. To be ridden, a bicycle must be moving, and to lead, a person must be growing. But growth is a complex process.

Growth Means Change

The basics are simple. The Bible sees the Christian life as a pilgrimage that goes from "here" to "there" through an experience of sanctifying change. Hence, to grow means

- to be conformed to Christ, Romans 8:29, 2 Corinthians 3:18
- to experience God's "good work," Philippians 1:6
- to be transformed, Romans 12:2
- to abound more and more, 1 Thessalonians 4:1
- to press on, Philippians 3:10–15
- to mature in Christ, Colossians 1:28
- to grow up into Christ, Ephesians 4:14–15
- to desire the Word, 2 Peter 2:2
- to grow in grace, 2 Peter 3:18
- to be progressively sanctified, 1 Thessalonians 5:23

and that equals change! If God has His way, we will undergo a divine-human encounter aimed at adjusting us to His agenda. A crusty old western preacher used to say that we can travel to heaven on the highway of growth and blessing, or God will drag us through every briar patch and mud puddle between here and glory!

But the growth theme has become so familiar that most of us can talk a good line while remaining pretty much as we are. We say we want to grow, may even persuade ourselves that we are growing, yet we remain static. Resolves to pray more, read the Bible more, give more, witness more, make little difference.

Then, by the grace of God, we may be led to Evalyn Christenson's book with its probing prayer *Lord, Change Me* or Larry Crabb's *Change From the Inside Out*. Both are guided tours of self-inspection that uncover the challenge of real growth.[2] We learn, sooner or later, that God's kind of growth is time consuming and difficult, requiring hard work and honesty. Self-satisfaction and smugness must give way to tough self-scrutiny. God Himself must probe and push, lest we remain one-dimensional and shallow. A friend who came to Christ in mid-life and underwent a jarring experience of growth threatened (only half in jest) to title his first book *How I Survived the New Birth!*

Growth means change. The Bible tells us so, and experience confirms it. But be warned! The "human potential movement," wedded to New Age thinking, is in high gear. Many experts are telling all who will listen how to "be everything you ever wanted to be." To follow their lead is to risk personal and spiritual damage. God's program, on the other hand, is good, and safe. He knows where we're going, how to get there, and which processes to use along the way.

Servant Leaders Are Changing People

Christian leaders, whether aspiring or in place, must be measured by a critical standard: Are they changing and growing? Is concrete, measurable, and balanced progress visible to others?

No one could say it more clearly than Paul in 1 Timothy 4:11–16. Writing to his young preacher friend, he says in plain words that as Timothy grows, he will lead. Follow his thought flow.

- Don't let people demean you because you're young.
- Model Christian character and behavior.
- Give earnest attention to your public duties.
- Don't neglect your spiritual gifts.

Cultivate these things! Give them full attention.

That's a pretty stiff assignment! Timothy is facing nothing less than an agenda for real change—personal, professional, and spiritual. And if Paul's recipe is followed, two results will follow. First, Timothy's growth will be visible (4:15). As one paraphrase puts it, "People will see you mature right before their eyes." Moreover, he will "save" both himself and his hearers. Since Timothy and his people are already saved, the words hardly refer to salvation in the sense of 2 Timothy 1:9 or Titus 3:5. The more likely implication is that both will be saved from spiritual and moral shipwreck (1:18–20).[3]

First Timothy 3 and Titus 1 subtly express the same truth. Gene Getz in *The Measure of a Man* notes that these passages contain twenty leadership qualifications, all of them called into service when selecting elders and deacons.[4] But the qualifications cannot be fulfilled by static, nongrowing people. Think about the phrase "husband of one wife" (literally, a "one-woman man"). How shall we assess that virtue? It seems to take us beyond the questions of divorce, polygamy, a second marriage, or infidelity and into an examination of the *quality* of the marriage and family life. Have the husband and wife truly become one? Does the marriage work? Does it fulfill the biblical ideal?[5] It is conceivable that a man who has been married only once could fall short.

Similar challenges confront us at each point. Try defining "temperate" and "sober-minded," and you end up describing a kind of person, not just an observable behavior. Elders must be hospitable, but is there anything worse than the "hospitality" of one who does not wish, or care to learn how, to *be* hospitable (1 Peter 4:9–10)?

I have long been convinced that these qualifications must be set within a framework of continuous growth, for they are more than a series of rigid benchmarks. They are a cluster of virtues to which all may aspire but which no one ever outgrows. They form a track on which anyone can run, but on which leaders should be continually out ahead.

If we see the qualifications in any other context, we run the risk of discouraging young Christians. They look at the list and are intimidated. Or they may conclude that when one becomes a leader, he has made it. He has reached the top and is now part of the elite.

Wholesome followership is the result of growing leaders. How great it is when a congregation can say, "Our pastor is growing, and we can see it."

A personal friend, respected by his colleagues, had twenty-five years of pastoral ministry behind him. Soon after arriving on a new field, he began reporting surprising progress. Excitement was in the air. The board was facing issues, taking risks and, along with their pastor, was leading the people forward. When I asked for an explanation he didn't tell me about his programs, a fresh church growth strategy, or some dramatic new leadership skill. The answer, quite simply, was a commitment on the part of pastor and people to take seriously the issue of growth.

As my friend worked his way through the candidating process, church leaders acknowledged they had grown static and that change was necessary. With refreshing honesty, my friend replied, "I, too, have been in a bit of a rut. I need to make some changes. Why don't we change together." Is it any wonder the church is off and running?

Glitches in the System

Sometimes there are glitches in the system. We fail to grow or we fail to grow as we ought.

Deceptive Growth

It's easy to assume we're "growing" when all we're doing is re-arranging the furniture. If, in spite of our professions, real change isn't happening, the problem is phantom or deceptive growth. James must have had something like this in mind when he warned of "hearing" the Word and not "doing" it. How easy to look in the mirror, ignore what we see, and go our way.

We encourage deceptive growth when we pressure people to do more while ignoring the being; to take more assignments because "Christians need to keep busy"; to conform to one more batch of external behavioral codes. And if we aren't watchful, we who lead may find ourselves on the same merry-go-round.

The result is stagnation, a malady Christian leaders find remarkably easy to disguise. We've been schooled in maintaining emotional distance—warned, no doubt, in college or seminary not to make church members our close friends. This emotional distance helps explain the comment of a board member who described his former pastor as one who "made you think you were his best friend," yet "never invited you to his house."

We can operate from behind a facade for so long that neither others nor ourselves can ever be quite certain about the quality of our spiritual growth. *Deceptive growth can lead to ministry that is busy, dull, and marked by an aching emotional void. Leader and people keep grinding out widgets week by week but with little verve or vigor.*

Dysfunctional Growth

The term scarcely needs definition. We know that those who grow to adulthood in dysfunctional families often become dysfunctional people. Families tend to reproduce after their own kind, and certain behaviors cling to us "like beggar's lice on hunting boots."

The most visible of these dysfunctional behaviors are "poor self-esteem, passivity, perfectionism, explosiveness, addictions (not just alcohol or drugs but food and work), and sexual dysfunctions."[6] Scan the list again—carefully! I've known many ministry people who struggle with dysfunctional backgrounds. They are almost always intelligent, skilled, deeply committed to serving others, and often driven. They've been educated, have mastered the skills, and have grown. But their dysfunctional growth pattern has made it difficult for them to be fully functional in ministry, for those behaviors that cling like "beggar's lice on hunting boots" are often the occasion for ministry conflicts.[7]

All of us are broken people, and God understands that. He has come to heal us. But leaders must be willing to acknowledge their own brokenness, accept it, and actively participate in the healing process. God's grace is best extended through those who know they have been wounded and are being restored. *The ministry of dysfunctional leaders may be marked by spasms of brilliance, coupled with the feeling of being on a roller-coaster ride. Relationships tend to be effervescent and shallow.*

Distorted Growth

Problems also arise from another direction—imbalanced growth. The intellect may be exercised out of all proportion to relationships. Great stores of knowledge may be amassed while the nurturing of the body is lost. Or, we may be victimized by a warm fuzzies relationalism that has no biblical anchor point. An overemphasis on relational growth may starve the intellect. We may be enormously disciplined but be unable to roll with the punches. Our ability to see the wrongs of others may be sharp as a tack while our own failures go unnoticed.

Distorted growth happens for many reasons—the bent of our personalities, abilities we were encouraged to develop or overdevelop as children, the stubbornness of sin, failure to take advantage of God's provisions, and the pressures of life. Society sometimes greatly rewards those who achieve much at the cost of diminished personal wholeness. Sometimes the community is so pleased with the imbalance of our lives that we manage not to notice what we are doing to ourselves. *Distorted growth often results in ministries marked by scary extremes. Depending on the individual, the extremes may be in areas of theology, philosophy, methods, personal idiosyncrasies, or practice. The missing quality is balance.*

Where Change Begins

How does change happen? The process starts at the point of experience, when we catch a look at ourselves as we are, honestly face the issues, and resolve that things must be different. The Spirit of God, through the Word and the church of Jesus Christ, brings us to self-scrutiny, to a sense of spiritual bankruptcy. From here, we can begin to know real change.

Solomon points out an action step in his prayer of confession at the dedication of the temple. In 1 Kings 8:35 he pled with God to hear and answer prayer when "each one knows the plague of his own soul." The word *plague* means spot, stripe, stroke, wound, illness, or affliction. Solomon implores God to hear and act in defense of His people, when each person "shall come to know the affliction of his own soul."

These soul afflictions are different for each of us. For some, they are open wounds, easily seen, like an inability to stop cheating on a spouse. For others the blemish is not so visible, perhaps a willingness to entertain behaviors that violate an agreement with God. For still others it may trace back to an awful and secret abuse in home or childhood. Or the illness may be a more genteel flaw like pride of place, arrogance, love of power, money, envy of another minister or believer, defensiveness, or self-protection. Whatever it turns out to be, the affliction jeopardizes the management of our lives. It muddies our fellowship with God, keeps relationships off balance, and torpedoes our ministry efforts.

Soul Illnesses

Soul illnesses! All of us have them, have had them, or will have them. They are the common property of humankind. Like old Mephibosheth, we are lame on both feet even as we sit at the King's table. But while some of us know the illness of our souls, others do not. The challenge, you see, is to know, accept, and own the plague—to say, "Yes, Lord, the illness exists, and it's mine." In the words of Romans 7:24, to cry out, "O wretched man that I am! Who will deliver me . . ." The good news is that the blessing of God is available for those of us who own our illnesses and throw ourselves on the grace of God.

But that healing usually comes with the deep and sometimes painful involvement of Christian brothers and sisters who are mature enough to accept our brokenness and stand with us as we are healed. At least that's what Sam found out when he finally broke the tobacco habit.

But I must go back to the beginning. Sam was a young married man with four children, a farmer, dirt-poor, and an inveterate tobacco chewer—which may seem to be a minor problem unless you understand also that Sam was a very serious Christian living in the 1920s in a conservative community, and was a member of a group with many rules, one of which said that Christians don't use tobacco. But no one knew that Sam chewed, for he had kept his habit a secret from everyone except the family.

This state of affairs came about because Sam postponed concerns of the spirit until adulthood. Cigarette smoking was one of the leftovers from his spiritual detour. When he came to Christ, he knew cigarettes would have to go. But the nicotine addiction remained, which led to a struggle and a compromise: since he couldn't quit, he'd switch! He'd take up chewing instead of smoking. He could hide it better.

But that was no solution at all. Though the problem was masked from the eyes of others, it caused an enormous battle in his soul. Sam knew he was a compromiser, so he spent years trying to quit the chewing habit—as hopeless as his efforts to quit smoking. One day while plowing with a team of horses, he threw his tobacco into the furrow and plowed it under, only to grieve later that he hadn't marked the place so he could dig it up. He even rallied the support of his family by gathering them around him one evening as he burned his tobacco in the stove, vowing never again to use it, only to rummage through his pants late that night for a few snippets to assuage his raging appetite.

Finally, in a moment of despair, Sam read James 5:16. A light dawned in his weary soul. The recipe applied not only to physical illness but to *soul sickness*. And suddenly Sam was faced with a serious issue—was he tired enough of his spiritual disfigurement to go to the leaders of the church (who were also his friends), confess his trespass, make himself accountable, and ask them to be his helpers as he trusted God for victory?

I weep even as I write, for Sam's last name was Longenecker and he was my dad! I've heard the story so often, and I know how painful it was for this man. Long before terms like discipling, support groups, mentoring, and accountability were prevalent, Sam took advantage of all the resources. He drove off one day, bared his soul with several friends, asked their help and prayer, and won the victory. In the words of Solomon, he came to "know the plague of his soul" and took some giant steps toward integrity and wholeness. The Spirit of God, using the Word of God and the people of God, accomplished a great victory.

My dad was a leader prior to his crisis, but his leadership capacity increased measurably thereafter. You will also find it interesting that later in life he was ordained to the ministry and appointed Protestant chaplain for a new prison in Harrisburg, Pennsylvania. So what does it all mean? I don't happen to be addicted to tobacco, and perhaps you aren't either. Ah, but we've already seen that soul plagues come in all shapes and sizes. And the point is precisely this: if we aren't growing, maybe we're stuck at a point that is, in principle, the same as Sam's. If we are, we can avail ourselves of the same solution.

Conclusion

I stress the need for leaders to be growing people, to grow toward the likeness of Jesus, to grow in balanced ways, because my experience and the Word of God convince me that the battle is often fought and lost on this spiritual terrain. We take too much for granted if we assume that Christian leaders need no challenge on this point. Ministry failures often stem from easy self-deception, growth that is distorted and imbalanced, or a dysfunctional past that is unacknowledged and its effects unknown and unaddressed.

As the challenge is needed by those presently in ministry, it is equally urgent for emerging leaders. Today's leadership deficiencies will not be remedied by more frenetic training at the "how to" level. A single-track emphasis on skills and techniques, far from addressing the dilemma, may well mask our real needs.[8] Our primary task is *spiritual*—to produce worthy lumps of clay, ready for the kneading and growing processes that mold them in the image of Christ. Our primary task is not "to help ambitious men to the top or . . . make little men who have (taken) leadership courses feel bigger than they really are.

Still less is it to produce *führers*, either large or small. . . . It has much more to do with the *making of integrated people*."[9]

To be ridden, a bicycle must be moving. And to lead, a leader must be growing.

Reflection/Discussion

1. Talk to a trusted confidant, perhaps your spouse, and ask this question, "Am I changing?" Honestly assess your life. List those areas in which need to change.
2. Are there persons in your life God could use to help you take a necessary growth step?

Endnotes

1. Covey, *The Seven Habits of Highly Effective People*, 30–31.

2. Evalyn Christenson, *Lord, Change Me* (Wheaton, IL: Victor Books, 1977); Larry Crabb, *Change From the Inside Out* (Colorado Springs, CO: NavPress, 1991).

3. Ronald A. Ward, *Commentary on 1 & 2 Timothy & Titus* (Irving, TX: Word, Inc.), 74–79.

4. Getz, *Measure of a Man*, 16.

5. Ward, *Commentary on 1 & 2 Timothy & Titus*, 55.

6. Louis McBurney, *Counseling Christian Workers,* Gary Collins, ed. (Irving, TX: Word, Inc., 1986), 120, 199.

7. Ibid., 199–200.

8. Kent and Barbara Hughes, *Liberating Ministry from the Success Syndrome* (Wheaton, IL: Tyndale House, 1988).

9. Douglas Hyde, *Dedication and Leadership* (Notre Dame, IN: University Press, 1966), 97–98.

Relationships! We've struggled with them, wondered about them, prayed for them to be better, and maybe, as leaders, even wished they'd go away. But God made relationships to stimulate our sanctification and to have an impact on our leadership. Our tendency to think that caring about relationships is fine for the people person, while the rest of us can get along without it, is devastatingly untrue. If we are serious about leading, we cannot ignore relating. When reading this chapter, notice:

- the connection between relationships and truth,

- that leaders must learn to relate as they learn to grow,

- that the relationships shared by the people of God are unique,

- how some practical approaches can connect relating to leading.

• 10 •

Leading As We Relate

A church suddenly lost its pastor, but the search committee soon had an impressive résumé on hand, and, after a candidating visit, a new pastor in the pulpit. He was professional, poised, offered strong leadership and pulpit skills, and transmitted all the right signals

- church unity
- team leadership
- discipling
- evangelism

But defects soon cropped up, relationships went awry, and the man resigned—leaving in his wake a dispirited and divided church.

In due course another pastor was called. His portfolio was less weighty, but the first year signaled a different kind of ministry. Within months, attitudes began to soften and people relaxed. Unity was gradually restored and the church once more began to entertain visitors. A member of the church, when asked about the change, answered, "This man cares about relationships."

This all-too-typical story underscores the obligation of Christian leaders to nurture relationships. They are responsible for the relational climate of our communities of faith so that God can be at work through His people, manifesting His life, His love, and His Gospel.

"But where does doctrine fit in?" someone asks. "Are you saying that relationships outrank theology?" No, but God help us to avoid the trap of relationally impoverished theology, however sound it claims to be. Though doctrine and relationships are different, Paul connects them in Ephesians 4:15. Truth (doctrine) must be held in love (relational integrity). Can it be that Paul is trying to warn us against truth-less relationships on the one hand or relation-less truth on the other, telling us that the one is shallow and the other dead?

Authentic Christian relationships can flourish only in the context of Christian truth. If truth is lost, relationships amount to little more than human connections. If authentic relationships are lost, the faith lacks credibility.

I return to my premise. One of the chief priorities of a Christian leader is to nurture relationships. To fail here is to experience a weakened and even distorted leadership.

The Need to Grow in Christian Relationships

Some may question the need for a chapter on relating since we have just worked our way through a chapter on growing. Why can't the one produce the other? Won't good relationships be assured if we "grow in grace"?

It's easy to think so. I once heard a preacher say that if people would do what Paul says in Romans 12:1–2, the rest of the chapter (a strongly relational section) wouldn't be necessary. In other words, get right with God and relationships will take care of themselves—an idea Paul and the Holy Spirit somehow missed!

But this line of reasoning ignores an unsettling fact—relationships may often be more easily managed, in a superficial sense, when we are spiritually comatose. Life in the doldrums is marked by emotional distance from people as well as from God, which leads to stagnation and alienation, which leads in turn to shallow relationships. And in a weakened state, it's easier to just let sleeping dogs lie.

But when growth begins to happen, our battered relationships rise up to afflict us:

- the long-buried grudge
- the parent or child we secretly hate
- the person who hates us
- the church member who frustrates us
- the spouse we no longer love
- the self we no longer respect
- the God we no longer trust

Suddenly our relational landscape can erupt with a fury so severe that it threatens both our equilibrium and our personal identity. We know what the Bible says about the peace of God, the love of God, and how God's people are to dwell in unity—but it isn't working, and we wonder, "Why?"

Do growing people need to work at relating? Of course they do, and Romans 12 is not the only text that says so. Peter, writing in 2 Peter 1:5–9, speaks in similar terms as he compares Christian growth to a process of "adding" personal traits like virtue, knowledge, self-control, perseverance, and godliness, which would seem to cover almost everything. But then he appeals for two more—brotherly kindness and love!

Once again the relational touch comes at the close of an appeal to grow—a clear implication that growing does not automatically lead to relating. Both must be addressed simultaneously.

Since relationships are so crucial to ministry, they must be accurately defined. And if we maintain that biblical relationships are conditioned by

- the image of God in us
- redemption through Jesus Christ
- membership in the body of Christ
- the authority of Scripture

we must then accept their uniqueness. Thomas Kelly was right when he said that in Christ we are caught up in a new relationship, a new "life-sharing, and love . . . a disclosure of God" that brings a "disclosure of fellowship." We don't "create" it, we "find" it.[1] New relationships are formed in which the hurts, needs, blessings, and resources of faith are shared.

Good Relationships Are Not Necessarily Christian Relationships

Since Christian relationships are unique, distinctions must be drawn between the real thing and what sometimes passes for the real thing. Biblical relationships can be confused with:

1. *Natural charisma.* The life of the party isn't always good at relationships. Sometimes it's too easy to hide behind a glib tongue.
2. *People skills.* Important as they are, these too fall short of the mark. It's fun to work with people who are tactful and clever, but "being kind," "loving" others, and "forgiving them," is a different species of reality. A used car salesman reported that when he pretended to have an interest in people, they were soon ready to buy a car from him. Fine! But Christian relationships demand more than a grasp of Carnegie's *How to Win Friends and Influence People.*
3. *Natural chemistry.* It's great to meet people whom we instantly like, but Christian relationships rest on more than instant attraction.
4. *Cronyism.* A good ol' boy network doesn't usually prove much. Those who have known each other for years often don't know each other well at all and seldom talk of anything except surface issues.
5. *A need to be needed.* Close personal attachments sometimes develop because of a compulsion to rescue someone from bad circumstances or addictions. On the surface, it seems so right. But the connections are usually of short duration and can be destructive.
6. *Cultural conditioning.* Church growth experts often hold up the smaller church with its warm feelings as an example of healthy relationships. But a dogged tenacity to hang together in tough times may derive more from a common religious tradition or a shared community life than anything else. Both of these can be valuable, but they are not necessarily Christian. The Bible opens up a relational perspective that is different and experienced only by those who are able to share the life of God through the Spirit.

In contrast, biblical relationships:

1. *Show concern for persons* (Gal. 5:13–15). We live in a brutal and brutalizing age, but how tragic when the norms of society become the practice of believers. A Christian journalist says that the politicking in his church is worse than at the state capitol, which happens to be his beat. Politicians know how to play the game and generally follow the rules. But in the church it's trench warfare.
2. *Are nonutilitarian* (1 John 3:14–18; 4:11). In our throwaway society, relationships are often formed that are contingent upon something else. When that something else is achieved (or not, as the case may be), the relationship ends. But if the love of God in Christ is the measure of our obligation, Christian love goes beyond mere utility.
3. *Are mutually accountable* (Eph. 4:32; Col. 3:12–16). We are to be accountable to and for one another; we are to pray for, forgive, bear with, exhort, and counsel each other. These "one another" commands require that we live in such close connection that one believer can draw upon the help of others. Interactions should be so solid that believers can gently yet firmly call one another to account. Where such accountability is found, lapses will be few and recovery more rapid.
4. *Require loving confrontation* (Matt. 18:15–20; 5:23). Confrontation is loving, one-on-one correction, neither people-bashing nor polarization, but a willingness to bring things into the open (Eph. 4:15). To love yet speak less than the truth is to sweep dirt under the rug. To speak the truth yet not love is to hurt and destroy. To speak the truth in love is to confront and heal.
5. *Are nonmanipulative* (1 Thess. 2:1–12). How do we manipulate? Let me count the ways. "Look at all I've done for you, and is this the thanks I get?" Or, "If that's the way you want to play, I'll take my marbles and go home (or resign, or quit my job, or divorce)." Or, "My needs aren't being met. Don't you care?"
6. *Are tough yet tender* (1 Cor. 5; 2 Cor. 2:1–8). Years ago the Hastings Piston Ring Company sponsored a popular billboard advertisement showing a brute-tough Marine with bare, bulging, tattooed biceps, sporting a six-day-old beard,

on the sidewalk shooting marbles with a towheaded kid. The caption read, "Tough, But Oh So Gentle!" Christian relationships are like that.

Examples

Since relational leadership is scriptural, examples are found throughout the New Testament. Space allows only a sketchy overview, but on this evidence alone we can judge that Christian leaders are obligated to give relationships high priority.

The Master Leader (Mark 10:42–45)

Jesus and the Twelve were on their way to Jerusalem where He would be killed, but the disciples could think only about who would hold the chief seats in His coming kingdom. When the ambitions of James and John became known to the others, the fellowship of the disciples disintegrated.

What did Jesus do? He turned aside from the demands of the journey and took steps to restore harmony. He identified the issue that caused the problem, brought in into the open, and dealt with it. Not only were right relationships restored, but the disciples came away from the experience having learned some lessons about leading and serving.

The Jerusalem Apostles (Acts 6)

Grecian widows in the Jerusalem church were complaining about what they perceived to be a racially-motivated imbalance in the local food distribution program. I am impressed with the response of these men. They knew they had a serious problem and took wise and sensitive steps to resolve it. They did not scold the people for their carnality nor mask the issue by involving them in more church work nor call a mass meeting to update them on the fantastic growth of their outreach program nor urge people to "trust them." Neither did they assume that conflict was good and should be welcomed.

Instead, they took ownership of the issue, offered a solution, got the people involved in implementing it, delegated the task and requisite authority to perform it, and things were soon back on track. Key management functions were honored, but what we really have here is a beautiful example of relational leadership. The apostles followed the example of their Lord.

The New Testament Epistles

We owe Gene Getz a debt of gratitude for focusing attention on the Bible's "one-another" commands.[2] To carry the exercise a step further, survey the Epistles for yourself and note every single statement on the subject. The following "thought flow" will whet your appetite, even as it strengthens the argument for the biblical priority of relationships. The selected phrases are unidentified and sequential. They begin with Romans and end with the letters of John.

> Be of the same mind toward one another . . . love your neighbor as yourself . . . pursue the things that make for peace . . . let each of us please his neighbor for his good . . . when you sin against the brethren and wound their weak conscience, you sin against Christ . . . have the same care for one another . . . be of good comfort, be of one mind, live in peace . . . if you bite and devour one another, beware lest you be consumed by one another . . . let all bitterness, wrath, anger, clamor, and evil speaking be put away from you . . . be kind to one another . . . walk in love as Christ has loved us . . . let nothing be done through selfish ambition or conceit . . . let your gentleness be known to all . . . above all these things, put on love . . . may the Lord make you to increase and abound in love to one another and to all . . . a servant of the Lord must not quarrel but be gentle . . . speak evil of no one, be peaceable, gentle, showing all humility to all men . . . let brotherly love continue . . . the wisdom that is from above is first pure, then peaceable, then gentle, willing to yield, full of mercy and good fruits, without partiality and without hypocrisy . . . do not speak evil of one another . . . be of one mind, having compassion for one another; love as brothers, be tender-hearted, be courteous . . . have fervent love for one another, for love will cover a multitude of sins . . . this is the message that you have heard from the beginning, that we should love one another . . . my little children, let us not love in word or in tongue but in deed and in truth. . . .

There's more where that came from. Furthermore, as we sift through the whole of it, we're struck by an arresting fact: there isn't a hint that possessing a certain temperament or personality trait modifies these commands in any way. Can you imagine

Paul saying in Ephesians 4, "Walk . . . in lowliness and gentle-
ness, with long-suffering, bearing with one another in love—
unless you happen to be a choleric!"

Temperament patterns are designed to create welcome
diversity in what would otherwise be a hideously bland church,
but they are never an excuse for side stepping, minimizing, or
ignoring the Bible's relational standards. All Christian leaders,
regardless of personality type or temperament pattern, are under
the same obligations.

Chuck Swindoll comments on the gulf between sensitive leaders like those in the early church and the "tough-minded executive who is always in control, who holds himself aloof, who
operates in a world of untouchable, sophisticated secrecy." The
ones who do the best job, he says, "are those whose antennae
are keenly attuned to others. They sense the scene, get the
picture, read between the lines. They operate from that sensitive perspective which weaves wisdom and understanding into
a fabric of ministry."[3]

The Approaches

But how does the job get done? In a practical sense, how does
relating connect with leading?

Preaching Ministry

Pastors are often unaware of the connection between preaching and leadership. Take time to reread the Epistles. As you do
so, try to see them for what they really are, powerful leadership
letters. Preach them from that perspective, and you'll be amazed
at the new insights on relationships that spring from these
familiar pages. As you share your messages, you will be con-
structing a relational spinal column that can provide support
for other initiatives.

Strawberry-Plant Principle

When I was a boy, my uncle paid me a quarter per day to
crawl down the rows of newly planted strawberry plants and
clip the blossoms so the plants wouldn't bear fruit. He insisted
that the plant's energy go into foliage the first year, with fruit
bearing postponed to the following year.

There was a method to his madness. Strawberry plants left
to themselves send out prolific shoots, which take root and grow

more strawberry plants, and send out more shoots, until they form a veritable jungle.

Relationships often seem to grow just like strawberry plants. I learned, along the way, that when I build a relationship with brother or sister A, the relationship can extend from A to B, and from A and B to still others, until the whole group is touched. The approach can be fruitful and is effective whether women meet with women or men with men. Within a year or two, a cluster of people can come alive spiritually. By concentrating on a few key leaders, the tone of church leadership can begin to change. And through it's leaders, the tone of the church can change.

How you arrange to meet with key people will depend on community culture. Going to a local coffee shop works in some areas but not in others. In ranching and farming communities it may be necessary to meet at the home or in the field. Offering to help with work may be the way to go. Do what you must! Be creative, but make it happen! And don't try to go too deep too fast. "Deep interpersonal relationships," says Jay Kessler, "must begin on the surface and work their way in."[4]

Personal Vulnerability

But personal meetings, by themselves, aren't enough. Unless we are able to be wisely transparent, what ever growth occurs will be surface and lopsided. Relationships are redemptive when we are *vulnerable*. The word means being "open to criticism."

Pop psychology has given the term a bad reputation, but contrary to impressions, it doesn't mean telling every sordid episode of my life to anyone who will listen. It means being real. Among other ways, we are vulnerable when we:

1. *Are able to listen.* A man lost three children to cancer. As his last son lay dying, almost everyone who visited offered counsel, brought a book or tape, or explained what God was doing. He could hardly wait for them to leave. To just listen, in a moment like this, requires vulnerability.[5]
2. *Are willing to admit our own need.* We can't bear one another's burdens if we aren't willing to admit our own. But it takes "a healthy self-esteem and confidence in the grace of God to remove the mask that some of us have

learned to wear. . . . But masked lives produce masked responses and superficial relationships. . . . Open lives produce friendliness and compassion."[6]

3. *Being free to express feelings.* I tapped into a new level of reality when I came to the place where I could look my Christian brother in the eye, take him by the hand, and say "I love you and I pray for you."

A wise vulnerability on the part of leaders will do much to quiet the complaint of many parishioners that "my pastor isn't real. He gives us biblical sermons, believes the right doctrine, and does many good things, but he lives in another world." A relational church requires more than orthodoxy and homiletically correct sermons. Leaders who are real people, in touch with real people, must work at living out quality relationships.

Conclusion

The approaches work only if we are mature enough to build and maintain healthy relationships. If we can do that, we will carry a wholesome relational climate with us that will make the principles effective.

Dan Allender says that our relationships are an x-ray into the quality of our spiritual lives and of our walk with God.[7] John's first epistle supports that claim. Our responsibility, then, is to move toward mature relationships in our own immediate circles, so we can lead our people to be more competent in their circles. Don Baker says that the leader's role, like the farmer's, is to "create an environment . . . conducive to growth, . . . free of suspicion, tension, threat, anger, and bitterness, so that relationships can flourish," because "people are the business of the Christian community."[8]

Reflection/Discussion

1. Read Romans 12; 13:8–10; 14:1–23; 15:1–14 and make a list of all commands that deal with relationships. Identify the practical sections of Ephesians, Philippians, and Colossians and repeat the process.
2. Deal with relational ruptures in your own life. Go through chapter 10 again and review correctives.

Endnotes

1. Thomas Kelly, *In the Morning, Bread*, ed. Florence Taylor (New Canaan, CT: Keats, 1976), 308.

2. Gene Getz, *Building Up One Another* (Wheaton: Victor Books, 1976).

3. Charles R. Swindoll, *Leadership* (Irving, TX: Word, Inc., 1985), 52.

4. Jay Kesler, *The Strong Weak People* (Wheaton, IL: Victor Books, 1977), 19.

5. Mike Yaconelli, *Guide to Jerk-Free Christianity* (London: Marshall Pickering, 1991), 33.

6. Kesler, *Strong Weak People,* 19.

7. Dan Allender, *The Wounded Heart* (Colorado Springs, CO: NavPress, 1990), 153.

8. Baker, *Restoring Broken Relationships,* 56.

Vision! Many crave it. Henry David Thoreau said he'd give "all the wealth of the world for one true vision." For leaders and those who yearn to lead, vision is a priority. Is there a way to develop it? Can it be grown? Burt Nanus says so, and some of what he has to say echoes our current theme—vision is contagious! Aspiring leaders can catch it from those who have it. When you read this chapter, notice:

- the need to distinguish *vision* from *visions*,

- the definition of *vision*,

- the powerful effects of mentoring,

- the ultimate vision,

- how leaders use vision to empower the people of God.

• 11 •

Leading As We Aspire

Esther and I began our ministry pilgrimage forty years ago when we moved to the Deep South from Pennsylvania as rural church planting missionaries. Our work began in a small village of eighty souls, with another three hundred people in the surrounding farm areas.

To the east, the nearest town was twenty miles away. To the west, twenty-five miles separated us from a decent patch of civilization. To the south, we had to travel thirty miles on mostly unpaved roads before crossing a state border and entering another town. To the north were trees.

A clapboard structure, erected for general use, stood in the little village. Over the years it evolved into a community church building. That's where it all began. And the tale bears retelling for it says something about vision.

Visions

To be true to reality, I must begin with *visions* for I soon had a whole batch of them.

Numerical Growth

My first goal was to recruit more people for our church. Many who needed the Gospel were untouched. The ten to fifteen who attended morning services were a drop in the bucket, so I began visiting. And the number grew. Soon I was preaching to thirty-five or forty people instead of fifteen.

After a few years we were led to another church, and here too my concern was for numbers. Once more the numbers grew. Our congregation quickly grew from forty to eighty.

Programs

As the numbers increased I saw the need for new programs, so we launched a cluster of them:

- youth ministries
- Bible conference ministries
- evangelistic campaigns
- training programs
- a better Sunday school

And the work continued to grow. People came to faith in Christ, young people crowded the services, and the community was alerted that something was happening at the Chapel.

Organization

It also became apparent that our little church could use more structure, so we initiated an organizational phase. We called the Christians together and invited them to sign a statement of faith, which became the basis for a tentative membership. The writing of a constitution and bylaws was followed by the election of deacons, the preparation of the constitution and bylaws, and the filing of incorporation papers. We were organized.

I was proud! Of our people, of the leaders, of my work. One more vision had been accomplished.

Facilities

But there was more. The building was small and had little space for Sunday school classes and other groups, so we began a modest building program. It wasn't big or expensive, but we were excited. As we worked together, the project was done— with little paid help. People from the community also lent a hand and rejoiced with us. When we dedicated it, another vision was achieved.

More Visions

I was shortly appointed field director for our mission, and two years later, general director. Nine years down the road I was called to serve as a Bible college president, then senior pastor of two multiple-staff churches. With each responsibility I experienced new visions, and grace to achieve some of them.

Vision

But early on I began to see, beneath the *visions,* something much more foundational—a personal sense of *vision!* Somehow, somewhere, I had been led to believe that I could make a difference in the kingdom of God.

Personal Experience

As I reflected on all that had happened, I came to realize that this sense of vision was the fruit of those who had been my mentors. One of these was my dad. As a farmer, he went bankrupt during the Great Depression. But an experience that could have made him bitter became, instead, the occasion for new ventures.

Unlike many, my dad believed he owed his creditors, so he worked hard, saved his money, and repaid them. In the aftermath of his farming failure he had begun a new business that produced a modest living. On the Christian outreach front, he continued a ministry in the depressed areas of nearby river towns. I went with him at times and saw for myself what "mission work" was all about and soon felt a similar burden. Finally, at age sixty-five, when most people are ready to quit, Dad was ordained to the ministry and for ten years served as the Protestant prison chaplain in Harrisburg, Pennsylvania.

Dad was a person of vision. So was Pastor John. As with all people of vision, Pastor John shared his aspirations with others, including me. Only gradually did I come to realize the force of his influence. Without people like John and my dad I may have had some visions, but I wouldn't have known what to do with them. *Vision* has been defined as the ability to "create a focus." Any ability I may have to create a focus for ministry is largely due to those whom God sent along to mentor me.

Reflecting on the past, you see, changed my view of things. I discovered that vision is neither necessarily something we're born with nor something we create out of whole cloth. *A capacity for vision is largely the fruit of a nurturing climate.* Of course, some temperaments are more inclined toward vision than others—pessimists are rarely known as great leaders. And God seems to give a degree of vision as part of the giftedness of those He calls into His service. There are also ways vision can be enhanced.

But only recently have we begun to realize our debt to those who impart this invaluable gift. If there is one thing that will create or enlarge vision, it is to give attention to people who have it. Admire them, spend time with them, listen to them!

Confirmation

Burt Nanus, in *Visionary Leadership*, urges leaders to be in touch with those they lead, to build others into leaders, to avoid going it alone "like Moses descending from Mt. Sinai." There is no need that our vision be our own original idea. Often the best ideas "float up from the depths of the organization, but only if they are welcomed."[1]

Nanus is especially impressive when he talks about how to insure an adequate flow of visionary leaders for the future. Scorning the hit-or-miss approach, he says that "if millions of new visionary leaders are needed in twenty-first-century organizations, . . . leaving their development to . . . random processes . . . will lead to serious gaps in leadership, as already seems to be the case. Isn't there a better way?"[2]

His instructions to parents are exciting. Parents can help their children grow toward leadership by making sure they develop self-respect, by helping them "learn to learn," by being "role models." They can introduce them to the "great leaders of history, . . . can help them appreciate early in life that they, too, can make a difference."[3]

He speaks in a similar vein to educators and business leaders as he urges each one to "serve as a mentor to these future leaders. . . . Be a role model. . . . Seek their advice. . . . Help them learn and grow, and show your appreciation."[4] Nanus, speaking as a secular educator, says in principle what the Bible says on this point. Effective leaders confer vision upon emerging leaders through modeling, mentoring, respecting, honoring, loving, and appreciating people—in the home and in the church.

If the principles work in society, how much more vigorously ought they work among the people of God, with the love of God, the work of the Spirit, the body of Christ, and Word of God as our resources.

Visioning and Leading

Vision, if it is transforming and sustaining, must be shared. How do leaders create a shared vision that allows both leaders and followers to be moved by the same dynamic? Here we touch on one of the most subtle of all leadership functions.

Creating a Shared Vision

The leader is primarily responsible for defining the boundaries within which the vision-creation process takes place. This means answering questions like *who, what, when, where*, and *under what circumstances?*

Vision forming starts with a set of values that serve as the template by which to define the group's role. The "values package" is formed by sorting through the existing values but refusing to settle for the lowest common denominators. Good leaders choose the most powerful values.[5]

Since all values are not equal, each leader must take a stand both for and against certain values. The leader also brings his own values with him and cannot pretend that they do not exist or are unimportant. He must clearly lay out the nonnegotiables. Pastoral candidates must be especially careful that agreement exists on values and beliefs before making a commitment. When the test comes there should be few surprises.

Values are basic to vision, but a vision is more than a set of values. A vision is an affirmation—succinct and action-focused—circling the point where values intersect with functions. A good vision is the result of a process including impregnation, gestation, and (sometimes painful) birth. And if the vision is good, the experience involves more than just a few people.

A Case History

A pastor, during his first two years of pastoral ministry, led his people on a "quest for vision."

The project began with a congregational questionnaire and was followed by a two-day board retreat. Advance preparation was done by the pastoral staff and board leaders. The program included relaxation, study times, and discussion groups. Workbooks were prepared.

Plenary sessions, led by the pastor, focused on Paul's ministry pattern as expressed in 2 Corinthians 2–4, with Philippians 1:6, Colossians 1:28–29, Romans 8:29, and 2 Peter 3:18 as support texts.

Group discussions translated the study themes into practical principles which laid the foundation for a statement of church vision. A core set of values was also taking shape.

A rough vision statement was adopted at the close of the retreat and in subsequent weeks was refined by a committee. The preliminary statement of both values and vision was circulated to the church, revised, and adopted by the board. The core vision statement said that the church is committed to "making a unique Christian impact upon people, by personally and corporately ministering the transforming grace of Christ to the points of deepest personal need, thus helping people change from what they are toward what God wants them to be." The statement went on to say that personal "change" begins at conversion and continues until we see Christ (Phil. 1:6). It called people to friendship witnessing, evangelism, and continuous growth, through the help of the Word of God, the Spirit of God, and the people of God.

The church now had a core set of values and a statement of vision, including brief references to its history and current ministries. Titled "Pattern of Church Life and Ministry," the document became the basis for writing specific goal statements for ministries within the church. Before it was finished, two years had gone by and all key leaders, as well as active church members, had been involved.

Keeping the Vision

Creating a vision is one thing. Keeping it alive and well is another. A group's long-term health rests not only on the leader's ability to create vision, but also on "the enthusiasm with which he communicates it, and the commitment the vision can uncover within the followers. This calls for leadership that searches deep within itself, and listens carefully to others, so as to help people link their personal aspirations together."[6]

Here is more evidence that servant leadership is neither weak nor aimless. To point a group toward a picture of what can be, toward a view so compelling that they are willing to challenge their assumptions and perceptions, is no mean task.

Conclusion

Visions, vision, and shared vision! And back of it all, a mentoring ministry. But the ultimate vision is the one that breaks in upon us as the shadow of Christ falls upon us.

This vision is dramatically portrayed in the well-known movie *Ben Hur*. Ben Hur had raced with the chariots. Now he follows a crowd in Jerusalem to watch a criminal die on a cross. As he moves along with the curious onlookers, stumbling and shoving, the Man bearing the cross comes near.

This Man's body is angled to the side, hiding His face. Only His shadow falls along the wayside. As Ben Hur fights the throng, the shadow slowly envelopes him. And just as slowly, Ben Hur's gaze circles outward and upward until his eyes meet those of the Stranger. The audience sees only Christ's shadow—and the incredulous ecstasy on the face of Ben Hur as he views the face of the Savior.

The transforming reality of Jesus Christ is the one vision that can hold us in those fateful hours when ministry is tested. More than that, if we go through life without this ultimate vision, we will lack a capacity for God's kind of vision.

Visions of numbers, programs, organization, and growth are good and I cannot listen to those who think meanly of them. But visions need the ballast of the vision imparted by our mentors, under the Lordship of Jesus Christ. A recognition of our debt to the body of Christ is essential, otherwise we can become vain, self-confident, and misguided.

Reflection/Discussion

1. Has any person, Christian or non-Christian, looked after you, cared for you, taught you, and mentored you? What have you learned from him or her?
2. Who are your mentors now? Do you have any? Make a list them. Are they servant leaders? What effect do they have on you?

Endnotes

1. Burt Nanus, *Visionary Leadership* (San Francisco: Jossey-Bass Inc., 1992), 167.
2. Ibid., 181.
3. Ibid., 182.
4. Ibid., 183.

5. O'Brian, *Industry Week* (October, 1986): 72.
6. Nanus, *Visionary Leadership*, 16–17.

You have it, the president has it, and your pastor has it. It may be vital or anemic, large or small, enlarging or diminishing, healthy or sick, but no one is without it. It is the leaders' stock-in-trade. I refer to influence. This chapter shows us where influence comes from, how crucial it is, what it consists of, and what to do to keep it healthy. We also learn that if our influence is defective, our leadership will show it. When reading this chapter, notice:

- how we define leadership influence,

- why influence is so closely connected with the four leadership qualities,

- how Paul's teaching in 2 Timothy is a reflection of the influence theme,

- how Pastor John's ministry influenced the life of a sixteen-year-old girl.

• 12 •

Leading As We Influence

A well-qualified pastor, six years in the ministry, remarked candidly that though his seminary training had helped him to study the Bible, prepare and preach sermons, visit, manage programs, and conduct funerals and weddings, he had not learned, and was not sure he had been taught, how to provide direction for a church.

Providing direction for a church is possible only as a sufficient majority of people choose to follow someone. But how are followers secured? People choose to follow leaders for many reasons, perhaps because the leader is

- a "big person" who inspires admiration, awe or even fear,
- someone who has climbed to the top and can make all the little people below him feel important,
- highly skilled and, as everyone knows, those who can are those who do,
- artful in developing a cult of personality.

But how do *servant* leaders secure followers? The answer comes in one word—influence! Influence leaves an impact wherever it is found and a vacuum wherever it is missing. But for influence to be wisely used, we must understand it.

127

Influence and the Flow of Life

Nature of Influence

To *influence* means, simply, to have an effect on others. But a careful word study proves it to be more complex. According to Wayne McDill, *fluent* means to "flow," *affluent* is to "flow back into," *effluent* is to "flow into." He suggests that influence means to "direct the flow of ones ideas and thinking into another."[1]

But influence involves not only the ideas and thinking of the leader, but *his very life*. Hence, to frame an adequate definition, we must say that leadership influence occurs when a leader "directs the *flow of his life*" toward others.

It's no secret that influence and leading go together. Authors in the early 1900s referred often to the connection. But the older definitions laid too much stress on the innate power of the strong natural leader. *Biblical influence is the fruit of a matured life, not the power of an overwhelming personality.*

Paul must have had something like this in mind when he called on Timothy to "make an impact" (1 Tim. 4:11–16). The Greek word *tupos* means to "make a mark." Timothy was to do this by his speech, his manner of life, his love, his attitude and spirit, his faith, and his purity—which required him to grow, build solid relationships, and apply his gifts. Quite simply, the source of servant leadership influence is a person who is believing, growing, relating, and aspiring.

But solid leadership influence requires that the qualities be balanced and dynamic. Influence is only as healthy as the person who projects it, and Jesus is the only perfect human example. Yet where these qualities are found—both in the secular world and in the church—you find leaders. And with the leaders comes influence.

Growth: Balanced or Imbalanced

When influence stems from healthy personal and spiritual development, leaders achieve great things like

- Joseph, saving people from starvation
- Moses, delivering Israel from bondage
- Joshua, leading Israel into Canaan
- Samuel, stabilizing the land
- David, establishing the kingdom

- Josiah, fighting apostasy
- Peter, preaching at Pentecost
- Paul, touching a world

At the moments of great achievement, these leaders were people of faith, moving forward, self-assured in relationships, and strong in vision. Yet there were other moments in each of these lives when the apparent absence of one or more of these qualities led to less commendable results, showing that it's possible to be

- a believing person but not growing, which explains why elders should not be novices;
- a growing person but weak in relationships, which explains the exclusivism of the "Sons of Thunder";
- a relating person but lacking in vision, which may provide an insight into young Timothy;
- an aspiring person but lacking in growth, which is probably the reason for the early failure of Mark.

Influence: Wholesome or Defective

The choice is not just between influence or no influence. One of the agonies of being a mentor is watching a protégé shoot himself in the foot. Disciples sometimes become vain, independent, resistant to nurture, and opaque rather than transparent. We need only reflect on the experiences of Jesus' disciples to see that they struggled with short attention spans, petty jealousies, infighting, limited vision, self-seeking, resistance, unreliability, the pride of a Peter, or the betrayal of a Judas.

Today one often sees the fruit of such negative influence. A young man, active in his church, loved to serve others. Since his ministry was so appreciated, he attracted a following. This following fed his ego, which caused him to chafe under the leadership of others. Soon he was the leader of a closed-off group within the church that followed its own agenda. As we can see, unless its wellsprings are pure, influence can divide and destroy rather than edify and unite. The solution? Each of us must make an ongoing and exacting self-inventory. "Am I, at this moment, believing, growing, relating, and aspiring?" Disciples, too, must be taken back to the basics. Fundamentals must be reworked and accountability must be practiced.

Healthy Growth and Influence

Healthy leaders provide direction through the wondrously refreshing work of the Spirit within a healthy family of faith, producing people who are believing, growing, relating, and aspiring, and who reflect

- a distinct package of talents
- a unique Christian experience
- a particular educational track
- a providential package of gifts

all of which equip them for a special place of leadership.

The "Four Ms" of Applied Influence

Influence can be intentionally applied. Seminars are available where a person can undergo an assessment of his or her personal style of influence and learn how it applies to his or her leadership ministry. There are also books and videos that outline the influence actions one can use to motivate people. For others, influence is learning how to move ideas and opinions along the lines of an established relational network. And of course, the delusion of power tells us how to influence by intimidation.

But I'm concerned with what the Bible says on the issue. We've already seen that 2 Timothy suggests a similarity between the leadership training methods of Jesus and Paul. Assuming that Timothy's diminished spiritual vitality was the occasion for this letter of Paul, we may also assume that as Timothy's leadership weakened, his influence waned. From this perspective, a study of the book uncovers some correctives that I call the "Four *M*s"—modeling (1:3–2:24), multiplying (2:2), ministering (2:14–26), and managing (3:1–45).

Modeling (1:3–3:24)

In the opening chapter of 2 Timothy, Paul calls Timothy to

- stir up his gift (1:6)
- banish fear (1:7)
- embrace the Gospel (1:8)
- support his mentor (1:8–12)
- hold fast the teachings (1:13)

- guard the deposit of truth (1:14)
- be strong in God's grace (2:1)

In chapter 2 Paul urges him to become

- a good soldier (2:3)
- a committed athlete (2:5)
- a productive farmer (2:6)
- a diligent student (2:15)
- a clean vessel (2:21)
- a ministering servant (2:24)

What a modeling challenge! Timothy is clearly called to model integrity—the quality Dwight Eisenhower said was supreme for a leader. If a man's associates find him guilty of phoniness, he will fail. His teachings and actions must square with each other.

Integrity has been defined as a "fine sense of one's obligations."[2] Beyond knowing theology and possessing ministry skills, Paul calls for hard work, courage, sacrifice, transparency, stability, strength, and accountability.

But integrity is not easy to come by. As Jay Kesler writes in *Being Holy, Being Human,* "On the one hand, we're called to be holy, to provide an example of righteous living for those we lead. On the other hand, we're human, unable to completely live up to our calling. How can we be ourselves, and make our inevitable mistakes, indeed commit our inevitable sins, without seeing our ministries destroyed?"[3] But being less than holy, he says, is "no reason to hide our faults. It's reason to admit them. If people watch us closely enough and long enough, either they'll discover what we try to hide, or else we'll crack under the strain of struggling to keep it from view."[4]

Integrity is crucial because it draws other virtues in its wake—devotion to Christ, an honest walk with God, holiness of life, a love for the people of God, and fidelity to spouse and family. I respond with gratefulness for those moments when, by God's grace, I was permitted to see the transforming effects of an integrity I was able to model. But I shudder to reflect on other moments, some no doubt unknown to me, when the zeal of friends and coworkers was killed in its crib because integrity was missing.

Multiplying (2:2)

Buried in Paul's modeling emphasis is the command to make disciples (2 Tim. 2:2). Timothy was sent to Ephesus to develop more leaders. His success on this point would be sure to enhance his leadership influence.

Think about it! A leader introduces someone to Jesus Christ. The convert is nourished. He grows, develops relationships, and becomes a person of vision. Skills are honed as he serves under his mentors, and in time he becomes a responsible Christian workman in his own right. Can this happen without enhancing the influence of the one who reached and mentored him?

A top-level executive, asked to explain his success, said, "I owe it all to the president of our company. He asked me, shortly after I was employed, to come into his office and be with him every day. At first I objected that I had no idea what his work was nor how I could help him, but he assured me that all he wanted was for me to be with him, watch him, and learn. I did as he asked and within a few years had learned everything the man could teach me. My success is the result of being constantly in his presence."

A Christian reads these words and thinks of Jesus and the Twelve, Paul and Timothy, Barnabas and John Mark. Multiplication is a key to leadership influence. The modeling and multiplying efforts of this unnamed executive colored not only the life of a young man but, for years into the future, the organization as well.

Ministering (2:14–26)

When Paul calls Timothy to be a servant (2:24), he reminds him to

- shun worthless "babblings" (2:16)
- pursue righteousness, faith, love, peace (2:22)
- "avoid foolish . . . questions" (2:23)
- not "strive" but be "gentle" (2:24)
- be patient (2:24)
- minister in "meekness" (2:25)

Servant leaders serve the babblers, those in error, the impure, the opposers, as well as the responsive. Read the words again and you will hear an echo of Mark 10:42–45, "he who would be great among you must be your servant."

Servanthood, especially in the context of leadership, is a tricky piece of business. I used to visualize a continuum that began with master and extended to slave. Along the way, I tried unsuccessfully to find an appropriate nesting place.

God has a better idea. In the Upper Room, Jesus assumed a servant's role without surrendering His authority (John 13). Though a servant, He was wholly conscious of Himself, His circumstances, and His work (13:1–4), even as He assumed the functions of teacher and disciplinarian (13:4–38). But from start to finish, He was a leader. By taking on the roles of both master and slave, He shows that servanthood and authority are compatible, not contradictory.

Servanthood is the fruit of the mind (attitude) of Christ. We can as surely be servants when confronting erring believers as when stooping to comfort dying saints. What matters is the spirit with which we do it. The servant attitude can't be taken on and off like a cloak.

If we're really servants, our influence will be felt; those who follow will know that we care, and will be more inclined to follow. Someone has said that people don't care how much we know until they know how much we care.

Managing (3:1–4:5)

In the last section Paul reminds Timothy of the need to manage his ministry. Timothy must preach the word (4:2), watch (4:5), and fulfill his ministry (4:5). The NIV reads, "discharge the duties of your ministry." In other words, do your work, do it well, don't slough off, don't cut corners, watch your step!

The roots of ministry problems often go back to the minister. With unusual candor, a church board chairman wisely yet bluntly rebuked a careless young pastor, "You know, if you could ever give a good, hard kick in the pants to the fellow who causes most of your grief, you wouldn't be able to sit down for a week!"

Ill-conceived plans, careless etiquette, and slovenly work will be endured only so long. "But what do you expect," someone asks, "perfection?" No! I ask only for the attitude displayed by one young man as he began to pastor a small country church. In his early twenties and fresh out of college, he was called to lead a church of older people, some old enough to be his parents or grandparents. He decided to be honest. Acknowledging his youth and inexperience, he asked for help. He promised to talk with them, listen, and take their counsel whenever possible. He would learn even as he sought to become their leader. As a result, the congregation accepted him, trusted him, and in time, followed him.

If I am a believing, growing, relating, and aspiring person, I will have influence. But that influence can be enhanced and guided as I work at the "Four *M*s"—modeling, multiplying, ministering and managing.

1. Modeling is leadership validating itself.
2. Multiplying is leadership fashioning its future.
3. Ministering is leadership pouring out its life.
4. Managing is leadership conserving its strength.

Knowing It When We See It

Ruth Senter, author, educator, and lecturer, grew up in Pastor John's church. Her dad was one of John's assistants and she was one of his teenagers. As she shared her reflections of Pastor John, she spoke of his vision, a vision of Christ's love changing lives in a little river town and how his dream took form in an old roller rink "behind the community center." Though unable to attend the funeral, she visualized it—the "white-pillared church" with a congregation of nearly 1000, "packed for the service" as her dad would say good-bye to his friend.[5]

But most of all, Ruth spoke of John's impact on her life! "Pastor John loved this pastor's daughter," she said. And even more, "he gave her a ministry. . . . He asked her to play the tiny spinet organ when the regular organist couldn't be there." So, at age sixteen, Ruth writes, "I probably became the first church organist in the world who did not know what to do with foot pedals. But I learned. . . . Pastor John had given me a job to do. And every time I played, he'd put his arm around me and say, 'Ruth Ann, you were terrific. Thanks for helping us out.' How did he know how much I needed to have someone think I was terrific?"

Sometimes, Ruth reminds us, people come into our lives and leave their touch without our knowing it until they're gone. Pastor John is gone now. "The phone call came this morning.

He died like he lived, 'I love you' on his lips. I will shed my tears. For in this day, when ministry has so often deteriorated to a high-powered climb to the top, it is a priceless treasure to have the memory of a pastor who whispered from his deathbed, 'I love you.'"

Her concluding words are memorable: "I am inspired to continue on in ministry, for he has shown me what loving service can be."

The man Ruth describes was known for his balance. Though rich and warm, his emotions never ran amok. His concern for people did not immobilize his commitment to wise and sensitive management. His impact was felt at both conceptual and feeling levels. So it isn't surprising that John's ministry produced leaders.

But it is surprising, I think, that his ministry didn't spawn a group of little Johns who tried to re-create him. I was well acquainted with John and his associates over a period of more than twenty-five years, and there was none who became a clone. John allowed people to become what God wanted them to be. He didn't foster a cult of personality.

How do we recognize the influence of a servant leader when we see it? Consider its effects! As Ruth herself intimates, she was

- helped toward maturity as John affirmed her as a person,
- strengthened relationally as John showed her the reality of Christian love,
- empowered for ministry as John helped unleash her gifts and abilities,
- molded by an authentic model as John lived out his faith over a lifetime,
- vocationally fulfilled as John allowed her to become what God intended her to be.

Multiply that effect hundreds of times over, and you learn what wholesome influence can be. You can also understand how a servant leader provides direction for a church. John validated his leadership through modeling, fashioned the future by multiplying, poured out his life by ministering, and conserved the strength of leadership through wise management. As a result, people shared his vision, and together, John and his people followed it.

One final note! John was a hometown boy. He earned leadership influence among those who were his peers. His closest ministry associates had known him from his youth. So far as these men were concerned, John wasn't seen as a great leader. Russell Krabill notes that, as a boy, John was "quiet" and "somewhat introverted," which only proves what every body knew— John grew! It was an ordinary growing, relating, and aspiring man whom John's associates chose to follow, and who eventually exercised remarkable leadership influence.

Conclusion

While John always took his work seriously, he never took himself too seriously. Hence, his people never put him on a pedestal. Had they tried it, he wouldn't have allowed it. He knew that effective mentoring requires a rare unselfconsciousness. As the "Four *M*s" are intentionally lived out, the processes must be natural and unconstrained. We are convincingly credible when the impetus for influence comes from the inside. Only those who have gone through Jesus' leadership development program can maintain simplicity while applying intentional influence.

Reflection/Discussion

1. Using concordances, word study texts, or translations, dig out the meaning of *example* in 1 Timothy 4:12. Why can we say that it implies personal influence?
2. If you are believing, growing, relating, and aspiring, you already have influence. By acting wisely, your influence can be increased. Talk with a friend and discuss ways you can better apply the "Four *M*s."

Endnotes

1. Wayne McDill, *Making Friends for Christ* (Nashville: Broadman Press, 1979), 53.

2. Max DePree, *Leadership Is an Art.*

3. Jay Kesler, *Being Holy, Being Human* (Irving, TX: Word, Inc., 1988), 15.

4. Ibid., 40.

5. Ruth Senter, *Power for Living* (Wheaton, IL; Scripture Press, 23 May 1993).

About forty years ago a husband and wife entered cross-cultural missions ministry. Don was a navy man and a product of the Navigators, so he went to his field with a priority to grow leaders. He was a church planter and was good at it. He was an effective witness for Christ. He was the father of five, and his fathering task was not ignored. And even with all his other tasks, after one term of service he left a functioning church with a group of men equipped to lead it. He went back for three more terms, strengthened the work and planted other churches. He has now retired, but the men he mentored are shaping history—at home and in the world.

It is the theme of this book that pastors in North America can do the same thing and that as we do so, good things will happen. When reading this chapter, notice how things tie together:

- mentoring leaders and personal nurture,

- mentoring leaders and church renewal,

- mentoring leaders and significance,

- mentoring leaders and tomorrow.

• 13 •

The Payoff

What Jesus *said* about leadership is revolutionary, but the record of what He *did* is the greatest of all leadership legacies. And the most astonishing insight to emerge from that legacy is the light it sheds on the object of His leadership—twelve ordinary men.

Were He someone other than who He is, He might have attempted to play to the fickle multitudes, but instead He invested His leadership almost entirely in individuals. And of those whose lives He touched, an extraordinary amount of effort was spent in growing just twelve leaders.

This example of Jesus' leadership priorities convinces me that what matters is people, and that leadership mentoring deserves to be the centerpiece of our ministries.

But leadership mentoring also has an intensely practical side. When it is placed at the center, other important facets fall into their natural places, and we begin realizing the potentials of being servant leaders.

People who are growing tend to be excited about God, serious about the Christian life, positive instead of negative, focused on the future, and loving instead of squabbling. Their self-concepts become more healthy and their attitudes improve. They are leadable. Pastors who hold a finger to the wind to see how many are "for" or "against" are missing the boat. Minister to everyone, but rest your case with the "becomers." They are more easily led!

Pastors of smaller churches can be encouraged by their unique productivity. John MacArthur, addressing a group of pastors, asked how many served congregations of one hundred. About a hundred responded. "All your churches together," said MacArthur, "equal the size of Grace Church." MacArthur then asked the pastors how many missionary and vocational personnel their churches had produced, and he pointed out that the number exceeded that of Grace Church.

A consistent focus on people lies at the heart of true servant leadership, and in the long run, this approach pays off in surprising ways.

Significance That Matters

People really are the key to ministry. The one thing I can do, whether my church is large or small, is help others become what God wants them to be. This is what gets me up in the morning and keeps me going—the awareness that God can use me to make a difference in the lives of people. Preaching, teaching, witnessing, small group ministries, leading, and managing are the instruments through which God applies this grace, but people are the focus.

This focus was on the heart of Paul as he wrote, "Him we preach, warning every man and teaching every man in all wisdom, that we may present every man perfect in Christ Jesus. To this end I also labor, striving according to His working which works in me mightily" (Col. 1:28–29).

Beware of Comparisons

If we struggle with ministry significance, it probably means that we're living with some kind of identity crisis—an experience many of us have struggled with longer than we care to admit. In contrast to a time when pastors were looked upon as community leaders, we barely outrank used car salespeople on the scale of respect.

Relying on ministry statistics—wealth, scope, numbers, prestige, and achievements—is not wise. The danger here is that someone down the road may have a ministry that is richer, larger, more prestigious, and more successful than mine. And if by chance I reach the pinnacle of my profession, significance may still elude me.

Despite the dangers, this is the path most often taken. Check out sports, Wall Street, education, main street businesses, and the board rooms, and you'll find it everywhere—even on your friendly golf course. Poet Ogden Nash, with a few humorous and insightful lines, wrote of the golfer's "pride of rank."

> Oh, where this side of the River Styx
> Will you find an equal mate,
> To the scorn of a man with a seventy-six
> For a man with a seventy-eight?
> I'll tell you a scorn that mates it fine,
> As the welkin mates the sun:
> The scorn of the man with a ninety-nine
> For him with a hundred and one.

Where do we look for significance? How do we escape being nobodies? In searching for popularity can we miss the most important work we'll ever do?

Who, for example, were the people praying in the basement of the Metropolitan Tabernacle every Sunday while C. H. Spurgeon preached? Who visited Dwight L. Moody at a shoe store and spoke to him about Christ? Who was Harry Ironside's associate pastor? Who financed William Carey's ministry to India? Who helped Charles Wesley get started writing hymns? Who taught G. Campbell Morgan his pulpit techniques? Who were the parents of the godly prophet Daniel?

These people were unknown, but they were not insignificant. They filled God's niche, did His bidding, and altered history. And whatever the size of our churches or the scope of our ministries, if we remain faithful to our focus, we too can be people of significance and reproduce others like ourselves.

Focus on People

Begin by setting an example. Make it a habit to touch base with three key men each week. Whether you meet in a local cafe, a home, or the church, get together. Relationships take time. Tell your men that you want to keep growing, and that you need them to help you. Don't come off as the Mr. Fix It man.

As circumstances allow, be transparent. I remember one

evening when a church board meeting had concluded and I was asked to pray, but an unresolved people-issue left me too emotional to respond. Two years later a board member asked me if I knew the point at which he began taking my leadership seriously? I didn't. "It was the night you broke down in a board meeting," he replied. "I decided I better learn what makes you tick."

Tears must never be used as a weapon, but neither does the cold, aloof executive pose the answer. Painful growth, at real pressure points, usually traces back to a moment of openness between two or more earnest believers.

If leaders set an example, people will follow and will multiply. Concentrate on a few people. When these are far enough along, meet with others. Within twelve months, little clusters of redemptive relationships can spring up within the body.

So what produces significance? Our people-focus and the quality of our work. An old craftsman whose skill was legendary was asked how long it took to finish an oak dining table. "Oh," he replied, "I don't know. I just keep working at it 'til they come and take it away." Significance, for this fellow, was found in the quality of his work, not the number of tables he finished. It's not a bad principle to follow in ministry.

Leadership That Works

To be effective, mentors must touch base with people who want to be mentored. And the wise leader will begin with listening. What's happening? What are people talking about? Why? Are their concerns well founded? What's being done about them? How can we address legitimate complaints?

These concerns are neither secular nor unspiritual. Listening is a spiritual obligation, and relationships touch life with God as well as with other people. Communication is a Christian duty. As people renew their relationships with God and one another, churches can enjoy a fresh breeze of communication and motivation.

It won't happen all at once. Patience, wisdom, and courage are required. But as the leader works through the underbrush, people will take fresh growth steps, and the church will experience modest but positive forward movement. You can identify it by the following marks:

- honest respect for people.
- an ability to listen. Most of us are "lousy listeners and worse hearers," says syndicated columnist Tom Peters, because "hearing is about empathy." Peters warns, "If you aren't empathetic, . . . don't be a boss."[1]
- greater participation. Getting people involved takes time, but it's time well spent. Try an experiment at the next business meeting. Place a "discussion only" item on the agenda and let people talk about an item without voting on it. Get ready for a surprise!
- a new sense of community.
- the stirrings of vision.
- love that begets unity and unity that begets love.

Improved communication and relationships can solve many problems, for carnality isn't always the problem and spirituality isn't always the solution. There's a lesson to be learned here from the story in Acts 6.

When conflict developed over the distribution of food to Greek converts, the apostles didn't call a prayer meeting (they were already praying, 6:2–4). But as leaders trained by Jesus Christ, they knew the problem was poor relationships, traceable no doubt to poor organization and fed by poor communication. So they chose a leadership option. They took the people into partnership, allowed them to participate in the decision, assigned the task to a team of men who were able to do it, and trusted the body to support them.

The working principles stand out like bold red letters.

1. Listen to people.
2. Don't "spiritualize" every problem.
3. Take organizational weaknesses seriously.
4. Form competent teams to deal with big projects.
5. Involve the people in decisions.
6. Trust the body to do the right thing.

Recruiting with a Difference

Jesus attracted followers by teaching, preaching, healing, and ministering—not unlike the strategies we've just outlined. But Jesus actively called people to follow, and so must we. One way to do this is to employ the transferable qualities I've discussed throughout this book. Let's see them as four challenges by trading the four nouns for a few dynamic verbs. Instead of faith, growth, relationships, and vision, let's substitute *commit, change, connect*, and *concentrate*.

Call People to Commit

The lost need saving and the saints need activating. The methods to use are preaching, teaching, praying, one-on-one contacts, and friendship witnessing, backed by a healthy lifestyle. Joe Aldrich mentions "harvest opportunities." New attender and new member groups are helpful. The opportunities are almost limitless. I know of churches with productive summer sports programs. If methods are supported by lifestyle witnessing, a continuous trickle of people can be on their way to faith and commitment. Begin a "Prospective Leaders" file.

Call People to Change and Grow

A moment of commitment is not the time to tally up the prospective Sunday school teachers, ushers, greeters, youth workers, and new committee members in the pipeline. Newly awakened souls can be quickly discouraged by being thrust prematurely into leadership positions. Learning by doing is great, but first they must grow.

Let it be known that you're in the people-changing business. Growth groups, discipling ministries, and support programs are good options. And if you don't have people to lead the new ventures, form a new group and lead it yourself. Provide the opportunity and encourage people to get involved. You'll see the fruit in a new appetite for the Word, an interest in prayer, questions about the Bible and daily life, a desire for godliness, and a burden for the unsaved.

Meanwhile, watch for those who are growing—and keep your Prospective Leaders file up to date.

Call People to Connect

Growers need to relate with other growers. Any proof I needed was mine for the taking when I became involved with a group of Christian men who were struggling with alcohol addiction. They learned that one key to growth was open, direct, confronting yet loving relationships. They were "connected." As I shared their gut-wrenching honesty, I often wished my non-alcoholic friends could have been there too.

Earl Jabay, Christian minister and therapist, confesses that his own spiritual reconstruction dates from the time he came in touch with a similar group struggling with alcohol addiction. "I decided to become a student and sit at the feet of these (men). . . . I heard them talk a lot about pride, phoniness, a false ego, the big head, and the high horse. And not only that! They had the audacity to tell a man when he was indulging in luxuries such as self-pity, . . . resentment, and self-deception, to list just a few of their favorite topics."[2]

Most of us are not addicted to alcohol, but growth that brings real change is as easily stifled by gossip, gluttony, arrogance, lust, divisive behavior, anger, self-protection, and insensitivity, as by alcohol and drugs.

This is why I would gladly enroll every Christian in a similar group marked by equal honesty and a willingness to connect with other believers. It produces a climate in which people can discover a new dimension of body life. So, keep calling people to commit, to change, to connect. And as they respond, update your Prospective Leaders file.

Call People to Concentrate

Believing, growing, and relating persons need to become aspiring persons. To reach this last goal, leaders and followers should employ several vision-producing tactics.

Vision must be modeled. Followers catch it from mentors. Open the door to your life. Share your dreams. While addressing a college student body, the speaker urged his hearers to "latch on to people with vision, and catch it." Good leaders make it easy for followers to find and touch them.

Give balanced teaching on spiritual gifts using books like *Beyond Spiritual Gifts* by Rick Yohn.[3] An effective leader knows and uses his gifts, but he also realizes that the mere discovery of a gift does not guarantee either leadership or spirituality.

Use proven testing instruments to evaluate individual temperaments and traits.[4] But do not assume that a special cluster of traits or a unique temperament, in themselves, are proof of a capacity to lead. The tests may tell us where and how we can lead, but not whether we can lead. Tests are most helpful when they describe what is, rather than what will be.

Rehabilitate the practice of apprenticeships. Vision grows as believers have opportunity to serve. Pastor John did me a great favor when he asked me to preach for him, for he stimulated my vision.

As you concentrate on these concerns, vision will grow. And at this point, if not before, you'll need an "Active Leaders File." Some of your prospects are ready for serious ministry. And don't be surprised if unlikely people end up on the list.

Of course if we're playing find the leader instead of grow the leader, we're usually not surprised at all. We've already eye-balled the crowd, picked out the sharp ones, maybe even tried to figure out their gifts, and handed them an assignment. We know who the leaders are when we start. But if you grow them, you can't know at the outset that

- a "warm body" can become a board chairman,
- a sexually abused person can lead support groups,
- a former alcoholic can be a church counselor.

Gems like these come out of left field and surprise you.

Ministry That Produces Change

What kind of person are we reproducing? Obviously, people who are believing, growing, relating, and aspiring. But what does this person look like? Lawrence Crabb offers a word profile of what he calls "a continually changing image-bearer," a description so beautifully in harmony what we've been looking at that I share a few glimpses with you. These people

> . . . deeply enjoy God . . . They know in their deepest hearts that they have felt His touch. That touch increasingly liberates them to be more fully involved with others. The inevitable pain does not cause them to back away. . . . Their lives have quiet power (and) their . . . presence is felt . . . in a way that makes others want to live more nobly. They struggle, and sometimes fail . . . but they know what it means to repent from the core of their being . . . and to return to the God . . . through Whom relationships and impact are available. Their styles of interaction with God and others are as varied as snowflakes. But one thing they have in common: a growing ability to be touched by God, and to touch others.[5]

Crabb's "image bearer" and the believing, growing, relating, and aspiring person are the same. And the progressive realization of this profile is the key to growing a new generation of Christian leaders. Even those who don't become formal leaders may exert a strong influence and thus serve as informal leaders.

Commit to Personal Growth

Leaders who aren't committed to reproducing more leaders are little more than consumers—somewhat like the corporate manager whose passion for short-run profits blinds him to the need for investing in research and development. Servant leaders build for the future through a pattern of lifestyle mentoring.

So, what do people see as they watch us? Do words like *integrity, sensitivity, purpose, commitment, growth, servanthood, vision*, and *humility* come to mind? Or do they think of *shallow, ambitious, controlling, self-protective, distant*, and *career-focused?*

To end up with servant leaders, we must begin with servant leaders. As we concentrate on strengthening the church board— the area of greatest potential—with time, patience, honesty, humility, and diligence we can be God's instruments to meld them into a more cohesive, sensitive, and ministry-oriented group. Then the church will grow, and it will change.

A new pastor was just getting under way in a church that was recovering from a traumatic split. Within a month or two of his arrival, he asked the elder chairman to review the church directory with him and identify those who were qualified to lead but weren't holding office. The chairman looked the new pastor squarely in the eye and said, "No need to go through the directory. There aren't any."

But in four years, the nominating committee chairman reported that there were more leaders available than needed. Such a thing hadn't happened in recent memory. What was different?

Clearly, because the pastor had set the tone, had become an example, and had begun building relationships, the strawberry-plant principle took over and other relationships blossomed. A new small-group ministry helped. Most importantly, a new wave of leaders appeared because older servant leaders fostered community, created healthy small groups, and did lots of mentoring.

Who were these new leaders? A few, but very few, came from other places. Some were shadow standers, people who were not using their abilities because they didn't trust the climate. Others with obvious capacities, after nurture and training, were ready to go. Still others, who became respected and effective leaders, would not have been picked four years earlier. They were the sleepers.

Conclusion

Christians can grow, churches can change, and pastors can find significance—if they are committed to growing leaders. That's the payoff.

Is it hard to do? The work is demanding because all ministry is demanding, but it's not impossible. A commitment to grow leaders does not call for another ten hours per week on top of an already busy schedule. What is required is a change in perspective! The same tasks are done and the same ministries performed, but with an eye to the effect on others. Take men with you as you serve; spend time with them, give them opportunities to watch, to be there, to learn, and as you create the climate, leaders appear! The pieces flow together into a cohesive ministry stream. Once the premise is accepted, everything makes sense. The ministry of Christian leading is a life lived, a ministry shared, a vision transmitted (see Appendix 1).

Responses to what I have shared will vary. Some may be turned off. Others may find the ideas new but stimulating. Still others, struggling to apply biblical principles, may welcome some help. Many, I hope, will be able to say, "Praise God, this is what I've been trying to do all along!"

I do not flatter myself that I have created a new way of leading and following. As the writings of others have shown, it's been there all the time. But if a few fresh categories can help us better understand and apply the pattern, I'll be grateful.

A busy Congressman spent half a day visiting VIPs in a hotel dining room in Washington, D.C. Wearily lifting a half-empty cup toward the waiter, he said, "Do something with this! If I have tea, bring me coffee. If I have coffee, bring me tea. One way or the other, I need a change."

Our leadership "cup" has also grown insipid. We, too, need a change. Join me in a commitment to the biblical alternative.

For Reflection/Discussion

1. Read Joe Aldrich's *Lifestyle Evangelism.*
2. Read Larry Crabb's *Change From the Inside Out.*
3. Read Max DePree's *Leadership Is an Art.*

Endnotes

1. Tom Peters, Syndicated Column, *Chicago Tribune,* 2 February 1990.

2. Earl Jabay, *the god-players* (Grand Rapids, MI: Zondervan Publishing House, 1969).

3. Rick Yohn, *Beyond Spiritual Gifts* (Wheaton, IL: Tyndale, 1976).

4. Paul Benware and Brian Harris, *Leaders in the Making* (Chicago: Moody Press, 1991).

5. Crabb, *Change From the Inside Out.*

• Appendix 1 •

Designing a Pastoral Mentoring Ministry

A mentor is a "prudent advisor," says the dictionary. But as Ron Lee Davis suggests, the term is further clarified by a story in Homer's *Odyssey* where King Odysseus entrusts his only son to the care and training of his friend Mentor, while he himself goes off to war. From this relationship, Davis identifies the elements of mentoring as "wisdom, caring, and commitment to the training of the next generation." Tie this idea to the principles of Jesus' discipling ministry, and you end up with pastoral mentoring.

Distinctives

It may come as a surprise, but doing pastoral mentoring, and at the same time fulfilling the normal work of the pastorate, is not an impossible mission. Properly approached, it can be done without slighting other important tasks or adding five to ten hours each week to an already heavy schedule and jeopardizing the personal and family health of the pastor. And because a mentoring ministry has the effect of gradually enlarging the pool of leaders, it can even lead to a more manageable schedule.

My experience may serve as an example. I reentered the pastoral ministry after leaving the field of education, and for

the next fourteen years sought to practice the principles outlined here. During this time I was, successively, senior pastor of
two multiple-staff suburban churches ranging in size from five
hundred to seven hundred. The following information gives evidence that my personal, ministry, and family obligations were
met and that schedules were credible.

> Morning hours were reserved for sermon preparation. Minis-
> try commitments were honored in areas of staff leadership, board
> development, strategizing, programming, counseling, sick visita-
> tion, etc. Several conference ministries were accepted each year.
> Weekly days off were honored, and one or two week-day eve-
> nings were usually free. There were no serious complaints that
> my duties were ignored, that I was inaccessible, or that I was
> spending all my time with a few cronies. Physical, emotional,
> and family health was sustained. Pastoral transitions occurred
> in a healthy climate.

Mentoring is obviously not a crash program. The frenetic
pastor who tries mentoring as a quick solution to division or
lethargy will be disappointed. Mentoring pastors measure their
work in years, not weeks or months.

Perspective

When pastoral mentoring is discussed, the most frequently
asked question is, "But how do I find the time?" The issue is
largely muted, however, when we realize that many activities
already slotted into the pastoral calendar afford the best
mentoring opportunities.

Board and committee meetings, staff meetings, retreats, and
task forces are good examples. Mentoring and administration
go together.

Pastors often schedule weekly or biweekly meetings with
church leaders as a way of keeping in touch. These occasions
are ready-made mentoring opportunities. As the work of the
church is discussed, leaders can also come to know one another
better, open their hearts, and stimulate mutual growth.

Teaching Sunday school classes and leading small groups are
great mentoring times. Relationships can be built and personal
growth stimulated.

Don't overlook recreation, fellowship, and sports events. One pastor who came to town to help plant a new church was told by a Christian teacher in the public school that passes to sports events were available for ministers. When the pastor said he was too busy evangelizing to use them, he not only missed a chance to touch the lives of townspeople, but also lost a golden opportunity to mentor an earnest young math teacher.

Visits with church people, in hospital or home, are fruitful moments. Remember that mentoring is largely an intentional and wise use of relationship opportunities.

Pastoral preaching is another opportunity, provided we can get beyond the idea that preaching is just designed to impart biblical and theological facts. Remember the words of G. Campbell Morgan, that "preaching is truth through personality." While the biblical text is the only legitimate basis for a sermon, people must feel our hearts as well as acknowledge the biblical truth. We must, in proper ways, be vulnerable. If we learn how to be wounded healers, we can mentor as we preach. Effective pastoral preaching has a distinct discipling tone about it.

Worthy mentors view every activity or relationship as a potential mentoring contact—a chance to stimulate growth in others as well as in themselves.

Scheduling

Beside these ready-made occasions, mentoring pastors make time for their ministry. Breakfast or lunch at an area eatery is often the way to go. In small towns or rural areas, other settings may work better—like spending time with the farmer or rancher and even helping with his work.

These contacts can be enormously productive. If three weekly appointments are scheduled, and if the pastor meets with each person every two weeks, a half-dozen men can be mentored simultaneously. If we assume that some of these, within a year, may move out of a primary relationship into a less intensive mode and their places be taken by others, the number increases. Combined with the mentoring that occurs in more routine settings, this type of schedule can make a measurable difference in the quality of church leadership within a year or two.

The schedule will, of course, require pastors to miss some breakfast and lunch times with their families, but if men are deprived of this privilege because of demands in their work places, we can surely make a few similar sacrifices.

Effective pastors do their mentoring work along with their other ministries. Mentoring is not a substitute for something else. The mark of a mentoring pastor is his habit of having other men beside him whenever possible.

While balance is necessary, priorities are essential. The pastor who feels compelled to micromanage is rarely a good mentor. Those who do the best job are quick to empower others, to appoint task forces, and to turn people loose. They know the importance of getting agreement on the basics and having clearly understood guidelines, but they are not constantly second guessing their subordinates or checking out paper towel supplies. They focus on mentoring.

Our aim should be to design a ministry that assures the satisfactory completion of all normal pastoral duties, while initiating a mentoring ministry that, within two years, can begin to alter the leadership climate of the church. Think through the ideas outlined here, apply them wisely, and you will find the aim turns out to be realistic.

Questions/Answers

1. How are mentoring prospects selected?

   Look for the person who wants to be mentored. The question is not whether he has the look of a leader, but whether he wants to grow. While the person is often an active worker in the church, you may also find him standing in the shadows. Look for him.

2. How can the pastor keep a mentoring ministry from becoming the tail that wags the dog?

   Scheduling is the key. Allocate a predetermined amount of time. If your schedule is full and a person asks to be mentored, he either should be put on a waiting list or mentored by someone else. Occasionally it may be possible to make room by shifting an active mentor to a less active mode and using the open time slot for the newcomer.

3. Isn't mentoring somewhat like counseling and thus likely to become a threat to other areas of ministry?

Depending on one's counseling philosophy, the two can be similar. Unfortunately, long-term counseling too often becomes a dead end road that doesn't produce healthy, growing Christians on their way to becoming leaders. For this reason I had a tacit policy, as pastor, that if long-term counseling seemed necessary, professional help would be recommended. Keep in mind that a wholesome mentoring ministry tends to reduce the demand for counseling.

4. How does a mentoring pastor avoid the criticism that he is hobnobbing with cronies and/or merely creating yes men?

Keep your purpose clear, and pursue your purpose. Are you really meeting with men for the purpose of mutual spiritual growth, and not just because you enjoy going out to breakfast together? I have always made it clear that I would be glad to arrange a meeting with anyone if he understood that our meeting was designed to foster growth toward maturity. When the ground rules are understood, there are few complainers. It stands to reason, of course, that we must be honest. If we *are* using mentoring as a guise for creating a corps of yes men, we deserve the criticism that is sure to come.

5. Can pastoral mentoring really increase the number and quality of prospects for church leadership positions?

It can, and it will! Here is where mentoring and leadership connect. A healthy servant leader, who is believing, growing, relating, and aspiring, will mentor present and potential leaders without turning them into clones or creating a cluster of buddies who do what the leader wants. The fruit of healthy mentoring is a growing pool of leaders, fed by many different temperaments, backgrounds, educational perspectives, gifts, and talents. And as the board becomes more mature and competent, the health of the body improves.

6. How long should a mentor meet regularly with one person?

It depends on the variables. If we're mentoring a church officer, meetings may go on indefinitely. If the one being mentored is a board chairman and a new chairman is elected, meeting schedules may also change. The issue also hangs on the pace of growth and what God is doing in the person's life. One pastor met with a man, more or less regularly, for over three years. As a result, the man went on to serve not only in his own church, but as an administrator in a well-known Christian organization.

7. How can the pastor's mentoring burden be controlled?

Use others. The genius of mentoring is its reproductive energy. Remember the lesson of the strawberry plant? Mentors not only develop growing Christians, they also develop other mentors who develop even more mentors. Within a year or two key board members and lay people can share in the mentoring work. It happens quietly and without fanfare, but in time, the fruit appears.

Use mentoring groups like Sunday school classes and week-day men's and women's groups—but don't call them mentoring groups. The first goal is not to teach the principles of mentoring but to help Christians become believing, growing, relating, and aspiring people. Use this book as a study guide, along with material referred to in the footnotes.

Use apprentice ministries. As a Christian begins to grow and his gifts and talents emerge, find a mature person with whom he can serve. Though the pastor can maintain a loose contact with the emerging leader, the ministry supervisor sometimes takes over the primary mentoring role.

Use task forces—another form of mentoring. A task force is a short-term ministry group designed to take on a single assignment. Growing Christians, under the influence of older and more experienced Christians, can experience even more growth while they learn to minister.

8. How can a local church mentoring program be structured?

While it is important that pastors and church leaders understand and practice the principles and give careful guidance to broad ministry initiatives within the fellowship, structure should be kept simple. I have become convinced that a rigid program is the best way to kill a vital mentoring ministry or to keep it from happening in the first place.

9. Does pastoral mentoring apply only to small churches?"

The principle applies to churches large and small. The key difference will be the circle of people being mentored by the pastor. In smaller churches, the pastoral mentoring circle will include more lay people. In large churches, the circle will chiefly involve board members and staff.

10. Where can pastors find more printed material?

Review the footnotes throughout the book.

• Appendix 2 •

Pastoral Mentoring and Leadership Transitions

The leadership transition at Grace Church, referred to earlier, raises some intriguing questions: Does a mentoring ministry inevitably have an impact on leadership transitions? If so, how? Should the mentoring pastor control the transition? How tightly? And what about his role once the transition is complete?

Since mentoring is closely related to leadership, the mentoring pastor obviously has something to say about the why, when, and how of leadership transitions. But handling the process is a sensitive piece of work, and men who operate from within a biblical posture tend to work on a set of fairly well-defined principles.

The Leadership Pool

Before fretting about the transition, mentoring leaders work at enlarging the pool of leaders. They know that without competent, trained, and well-placed leaders at all levels, a church is not prepared for a healthy transition. Pastor Nussbaum's major contribution to the long-term health of Grace Church was the corps of solid leaders he left them. The success of the transition was proportional to the strength of their built-in leadership.

The Question of Confidence

Healthy transitions grow out of the confidence of people in their leaders and the ability of leaders to involve the church in the transition process. Something more is required than the personal desire of a strong leader to install his handpicked choice. Two principles must intersect—(1) a strong pool of leaders who trust the people and involve them in the process, and (2) people who are disposed to trust responsible leaders.

With respect to Grace Church, it is hard to imagine a setting where it would have been more natural for a pastor to pick his successor, and with little fear of backlash. Milo Nussbaum had served the church for thirty years, was respected and trusted, and Doug Habegger, the new senior pastor who would eventually be chosen, was already on staff. Doug was the son of close family friends of the Nussbaums and was known to Milo from the time he was a boy. Doug had the highest respect for his mentor.

But Milo went a different route. He announced his intent to resign and encouraged the church to engage in a serious pastoral search. The church contacted about a dozen possible candidates, several of whom preached in precandidating situations. One of them, Doug, was called.

The search process was not fake, and it reflected Nussbaum's confidence in the men he trained. He must have known that Doug would be a wise choice, for after working hard to build a pool of leaders, it isn't unusual to have a successor in the wings. But Pastor Nussbaum was so sure of the godliness and wisdom of his men and trusted so surely in the providence of God, he stepped back and allowed the decision to be made by the church.

It may not always happen this way. Resigning or retiring pastors may sometimes play a more dominant role. But tragedies occur far more often under the heavy-handed actions of dominant leaders than under the lighter touch of one who both has and demonstrates confidence in those he has nurtured.

The Retiring Pastor

It is usually wise for retiring pastors to leave the field and seek another church home—though I understand how hard this is. Pastors always find it tough to leave people they love and who love them in return. It's doubly hard to leave the last church one will ever pastor, but it's usually best to do so.

There are notable exceptions, among them John Hiestand and Milo Nussbaum. Both stayed in their congregations after retirement and did so successfully. But the man who chooses this course must master three very demanding principles.

1. *He must be able to bring effective closure to his ministry.* By effective ministry closure, I refer to an ability to (a) lay aside the sense of oversight responsibility; (b) handle the delicate balance of maintaining friendships with those to whom he has no further leadership role; (c) transition from the role of leader to the role of follower. If he has not mastered these principles before retirement, it is unlikely he can do so afterward.

2. *He must define his new role.* In Milo Nussbaum's case, he told Doug Habegger that he would do nothing in the way of ministry without asking Doug's permission—not even make a hospital call. And I remind you—this was the decision of the retiring pastor, not the new man. If this seems like a piece of overcompensation, it may suggest that the three principles discussed above have not been fully internalized.

3. *He must have the maturity and discipline to follow his own script.* This is not easy. Circumstances are sure to arise when one's sense of pastoral duty threatens to run amuck and mess up all the guidelines. Results of such actions are inevitably destructive.

I have come to the conclusion that if serious problems arise in settings where a former pastor has retired and remained in the church, it is usually the fault of the retiree. At John Hiestand's funeral one of his successors remarked that his pastor friends were appalled when they learned he was leading a church with a retired pastor in the congregation. "But you don't know Pastor John," said the speaker. In all the years of his ministry, John Hiestand had been a help and blessing rather than a problem.

In Summary

The value of a pastoral mentoring ministry, if rightly done, will be unveiled when transition time rolls around. Whether or not there is a successor offstage is beside the point. The church will be blessed with effective leaders who know how to involve the people and trust God to direct them to the one who will lead them through the next stage of their journey.